FEDERAL RESERVE BANK OF CHICAGO

UCHICAGO Consortium on School Research

I0215812

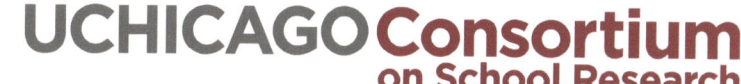

RESEARCH REPORT MAY 2019

GoCPS: A First Look at Ninth-Grade Applications, Offers, and Enrollment

Lisa Barrow and Lauren Sartain

TABLE OF CONTENTS

1 Introduction

Chapter 1
5 The Ins and Outs of GoCPS

Chapter 2
11 GoCPS Applications & Offers

Chapter 3
19 Where Did Ninth-Graders Enroll?

Chapter 4
23 The Types of Schools Where Ninth-Graders Enrolled

Chapter 5
31 School-by-School Changes in High School Enrollment

Chapter 6
33 Interpretive Summary

35 References

37 Appendix

ACKNOWLEDGEMENTS

The authors thank the staff at Chicago Public Schools, particularly the Office of Access and Enrollment, and the UChicago Consortium for providing access to the data and helping answer many, many questions. We had excellent assistance from Amanda McFarland, Avinash Moorthy, Cecilia Moreira, Todd Rosenkranz, Ini Umosen, and Connie Xu. This paper benefited from discussions with Elaine Allensworth, John Easton, Alida Mitau, Jenny Nagaoka, Jessica Tansey, and Marisa de la Torre, as well as workshop participants at the Federal Reserve Bank of Chicago and the UChicago Consortium. We also thank the Consortium Steering Committee for engaging with the research, including Gina Caneva, Raquel Farmer-Hinton, and Shazia Miller. The authors are thankful for funding provided by the Consortium Investor Council that funds critical work beyond the initial research: putting the research to work, refreshing the data archive, replicating previous studies, and seeding new studies. Members include: Brinson Foundation, Chicago Community Trust, CME Group Foundation, Crown Family Philanthropies, Lloyd A. Fry Foundation, Joyce Foundation, Lewis- Sebring Family Foundation, McDougal Family Foundation, Osa Foundation, Polk Bros. Foundation, Robert McCormick Foundation, Spencer Foundation, Steans Family Foundation, and The Chicago Public Education Fund.

Cite as: Barrow, L., & Sartain, L. (2019). *GoCPS: A first look at ninth-grade applications, offers, and enrollment.* Chicago, IL: University of Chicago Consortium on School Research.

This report was produced by the UChicago Consortium's publications and communications staff: Lisa Sall, Director of Outreach and Communication; Jessica Tansey, Communications Manager; Jessica Puller, Communications Specialist; and Alida Mitau, Development and Communications Coordinator.

Graphic Design: Jeff Hall Design
Photography: Eileen Ryan
Editing: Alida Mitau and Jessica Puller

05.2019/50/jh.design@rcn.com

Introduction

Student Enrollment in Chicago Public Schools: An Overview

Chicago Public Schools (CPS) offers many options when it comes to high school enrollment. In fact, since the 2015-16 school year, about three out of every four incoming ninth-graders have chosen to attend a high school other than their assigned neighborhood school.[1]

Among the options are schools and programs with lottery-based admission, which include the district's charter schools and Career and Technical Education (CTE) programs. There are also schools and programs for which admission is determined by application points, based on prior academic achievement measures like test scores or grades, entrance exams, interviews, recommendation letters, and/or auditions. These include selective enrollment high schools (SEHS), International Baccalaureate (IB) programs, military programs, and arts programs. Students can also apply to attend general education programs at neighborhood high schools that are not their own attendance-area school.

Despite the widespread engagement in school choice, the high school application process was complicated. In an effort to simplify and streamline the process, the Chicago Board of Education voted on April 26, 2017 to adopt a common application across all high school choice programs for incoming ninth-grade students with one deadline and a single best offer.[2] The district expected that this common application would make the process simpler, more transparent, and more equitable for students and families. At the time when Chicago passed this measure, similar systems had already been approved and were in use in a number of other urban districts, including Denver, New Orleans, New York City, and Washington DC.

The district's prior high school application system involved multiple applications, requirements, and deadlines. In the past, some applications were submitted to schools directly, while others were processed by the CPS Office of Access and Enrollment (OAE). Some students received and accepted multiple offers, while others were placed on waiting lists or received no offers. A motivating factor for moving to a common application included trying to reduce the difficulties students and families faced in navigating a cumbersome application system. Ultimately, the complexity of the prior system had the potential to generate inequities, due to differential family and school resources to support students through the process. CPS CEO Dr. Janice Jackson is cited on the CPS website as saying, "We cannot have a system that allows some people to feel that they can access it with ease, while others feel like it's too complicated and choose to disengage."[3]

The old enrollment system also created uncertainty for schools. Namely, without centralized enrollment, many schools did not know how many students to ex-

---

1 Barrow & Sartain (2017).
2 CPS uses the term "choice" high school programs to mean any high school program with the exception of the 11 SEHS programs. "Choice" programs do not include special education or alternative high school programs.
3 Chicago Public Schools (n.d.).

pect in the fall, making it difficult to plan for the beginning of the school year. With the introduction of centralized enrollment, the district and high schools would have a more accurate count of how many students will enroll. Given the importance of the transition to high school, schools likely benefit from being able to plan better for their incoming ninth-graders.

Beginning in fall 2017, all high school program applications were moved to an online platform known as GoCPS.[4] This new application system eliminated the need to apply school-by-school and program-by-program. In addition, all high school programs had a common deadline for applications and acceptances of offers. Importantly, the selection system alleviated the problem of some students accepting multiple offers to competitive programs while others remained on multiple waitlists with no offers.

The district distinguishes two broad types of programs — SEHS programs and choice programs. Each type has separate but parallel applications on the GoCPS platform. The application for SEHSs had been overseen by OAE for several years and had no change in the rules regarding how many programs to which a student could apply or the process by which students were admitted. In contrast, moving to GoCPS for all other high school programs, including charter schools, and the adoption of a system in which students were only admitted to a single program represented a major shift in CPS high school admissions. Much of our discussion about applications will focus on choice program applications, since this represents the largest policy change. We make note when SEHSs are included in the analysis. In particular, our analysis of school enrollment will include both choice programs and SEHS programs.

Questions Answered in this Study

The transition to GoCPS represented a major shift in how students and families research, apply to, and enroll in schools. While GoCPS certainly streamlines the application and enrollment process, this report seeks to answer a number of questions about the system. Who used GoCPS to apply to high schools? Did students receive offers from the programs they ranked at the top of their application? Were some student subgroups more or less likely to apply or more or less likely to get top offers? Did the process of assigning offers to applicants work as intended? For the first time, centralized applications provided information about the types of programs students applied to most often. What were those programs? Shifting to look at patterns in enrollment, some expressed concerns that neighborhood schools would suffer enrollment declines because GoCPS made it easier to apply to choice programs and charter schools in particular. At the same time, charter schools gave up some autonomy regarding their admissions process. Were there major shifts in enrollment—both in terms of total numbers and student demographics—by school type or for individual schools? Did students enroll in the schools where they accepted offers? Where did students who did not apply or who did not accept offers ultimately enroll?

The centralized nature of GoCPS allowed district policymakers and researchers, among others, to understand more about the application and enrollment process. This report provides answers to questions about the first year of implementation of GoCPS for students looking to enroll in ninth grade in the fall of 2018. Main findings include the following:

- Engagement with GoCPS was high. In fall 2017, almost all CPS eighth-graders (92 percent) used GoCPS to apply to high school.

- Most applicants received an offer at a preferred choice program.
  - Of all Round 1 applicants, 81 percent received an offer at a choice program that they listed in the top three on their application.
  - Applicants who did not receive an offer to any choice program applied to fewer programs on average and tended to be enrolled outside of CPS for eighth grade.

---

4 Many elementary school applications were also moved to the GoCPS platform, though the selection process worked differently. We do not address elementary school applications in this paper, and the findings here about high school applications, offers, and enrollment may not apply.

- Centralized information about demand for choice programs was available for the first time as a result of the universal application process. CTE and arts programs tended to be popular, as well as programs with points-based admission, like IB. Programs located at high schools with high accountability ratings were also in high demand.
    - As in prior years, demand for SEHSs was high, with about 60 percent of choice applicants also applying to a SEHS program in Round 1.
- Students were offered seats according to the process described on the GoCPS website. Seats offered at lottery programs appeared to be random, and seats offered at points-based programs went to the highest-scoring applicants first.
- Following applicants into ninth grade, most students who accepted an offer (80 percent) enrolled at the school where they accepted that offer. For enrolled ninth-graders who did not apply using GoCPS, many enrolled in a school where they had guaranteed enrollment (e.g., their neighborhood high school or a charter school in which they were enrolled for eighth grade). This is expected behavior for non-applicants, as students were not required to apply to their own neighborhood general education program.
- Overall first-time ninth-grade enrollment stayed relatively stable between fall 2017 (before GoCPS) and fall 2018 (after GoCPS). Ninth-grade enrollment by school type and accountability rating also stayed relatively stable. That is, neighborhood schools, for example, enrolled a similar number of ninth-graders in fall 2018 as they had the previous fall, and the share of students in high schools with the highest accountability ratings was unchanged. In other words, the typical high school had an incoming ninth-grade class that was similar in size and characteristics to the previous year's ninth-graders.
- Throughout this report, we show differences in application and enrollment patterns by student race/ethnicity and the socioeconomic status (SES) of the neighborhood where the student lives. Student subgroups differed in the number of programs they ranked on their application and their likelihood of ranking a highly rated school at the top of their application. There were also differences in students' likelihood of completing post-application program admission requirements, such as participating in an audition, interviewing, or attending an IB information session. Not completing one of these requirements made a student ineligible for admission, even if the requirement (attending an IB information session) did not affect their application points.
    - Students living in low-SES neighborhoods and Black students ranked more programs, on average, but were less likely than other students to rank a program at a highly rated school at the top of their application. This suggests that families may seek schools for reasons not captured by accountability ratings.
    - Students living in low-SES neighborhoods and Black students were also less likely to complete post-application admissions requirements. This suggests that some students may face barriers to enrollment in particular types of programs.
- Ultimately, GoCPS did not result in major changes in enrollment patterns by students of different races/ethnicities or living in neighborhoods with different socioeconomic conditions. It is impossible to compare patterns in GoCPS applications to prior years' applications since many applications were decentralized in the past. However, the GoCPS application data provide information for policymakers, families, and community members to use in conversations about access to different kinds of schools, as well as about what characteristics students and families value most in choosing a high school program.
- More research is certainly needed to better understand what families value and what students need to be successful in high school and beyond. We plan to study these questions as students and the district continue to use GoCPS for high school application and enrollment and as families continue to learn how to engage with the GoCPS platform. Once questions like these are answered, policymakers will be in a better position to deem whether or not GoCPS was a positive change for students.

Data and Study Sample

The CPS Office of Access and Enrollment (OAE) provided us with a number of different datasets in order to understand the application, offer, and enrollment processes for students entering high school in fall 2018. These included data generated by the GoCPS system itself, such as unique student identification numbers and basic demographic information, as well as students' rankings of programs, responses from the selection process, students' acceptance or rejection of offers, and detailed program information.

1. **High School Program Data.** This file contains a list of all high school options to which a student entering ninth grade could apply, including the program code, program name, admission type, program type, program group, grades served, an indicator for whether it is a SEHS program, and the school identification code. There are also indicators for priority groups and eligibility requirements, as well as program capacity.

2. **Applicant Data.** These data include unique applicant GoCPS identification numbers, as well as CPS student identification numbers that allow us to link students to other CPS administrative data. The applicant data also include gender, IEP and EL status, neighborhood tier, seventh-grade measures of core subject grades, NWEA national percentile scores in math and reading, and school attendance rate.

3. **Application Data.** The application data include applications for all types of programs, including an application identifier for each program ranked, the program code, program name, and preference ranking. These data also include information on whether applicants are eligible for certain priority groups, as well as application scores when applicable. Also, included are the program or programs the applicant is entitled to attend (e.g., their neighborhood HS program or a continuing enrollment program).

4. **Selection Data.** The selection data include the offer outcome for every program an applicant ranks. That is, we can see if a student was
   1. offered a seat at the program,
   2. waitlisted at the program,
   3. ineligible for the program, or
   4. not considered for the program because they were offered a seat at a program they ranked more highly ("higher rank offered").

5. **Student Response Data.** The student response file includes information on how students responded to their program offer. The data indicate if the student
   1. accepted the offer,
   2. accepted an offer elsewhere,
   3. declined the offer, or
   4. did not respond.

6. **CPS Administrative Data.** CPS Masterfile data provide enrollment data for all active students in the fall of 2017 (as of October 2, 2017), in addition to data on students who were previously enrolled in CPS.[A] We also used CPS Masterfile data from fall of 2018 to see where students enrolled in high school. Both datasets include information on student demographics (race/ethnicity, gender), free/reduced-price lunch status, special education status, and the school code for their current enrolled school.

A When CPS calculated statistics about applicants, they used an enrollment file generated in March 2018. As a result, there may be small discrepancies in the numbers publicly reported by CPS and the numbers that we report in this paper.

CHAPTER 1

The Ins and Outs of GoCPS

Students applying to enroll in CPS high schools in the fall of 2018 used the new GoCPS online platform to research school options, complete applications, learn about their application and offer status, and ultimately accept or decline admissions offers. All charter and district-run high schools and programs participated in GoCPS, including SEHSs and special programs like IB and CTE. The main exception was that assignment to special education cluster programs and alternative schools occurred outside the GoCPS system.[5] In total, nearly 290 programs were offered on the platform, including 11 SEHS programs. The fact that almost all high schools participated in GoCPS was an innovation. For example, at the time of this report, most other large urban districts did not include charter schools in their universal enrollment systems, as charters have traditionally controlled their own application process and lotteries.

GoCPS Application and Admission Timeline

There were two application rounds for fall 2018 enrollment, and **Figure 1** shows timelines of the GoCPS process for both. Round 1 began in August 2017, when families were invited to activate GoCPS online accounts and start exploring program options. Students began completing applications in early October, and program rankings had to be finalized online or submitted to CPS OAE by December 22, 2017. For programs with additional post-application requirements, such as auditions for music programs, the selective enrollment admission exam, and IB information sessions, students could register for these events using the GoCPS platform. These requirements needed to be completed during January and February in order for students to be eligible for admission to those programs. At the end of March, students and families were notified about their application results; they had until April 13, 2018 to accept or decline their offer. Students were also given the option of accepting enrollment at their neighborhood high school or continuing enrollment program at the same time. Students were offered at most one choice program and one SEHS program in addition to their neighborhood or continuing enrollment program and were only allowed to accept one offer.

The application window for Round 2 opened April 30, 2018, with applications due by May 6, 2018. Central office posted a list of 197 programs with open seats on the GoCPS platform, including four programs that were not posted for Round 1.[6] Round 2 was open to students who had not completed an application in Round 1, did not receive a Round 1 offer, or preferred a program available in Round 2 over the offer they accepted in Round 1. However, if a Round 1 applicant received a Round 2 offer, they forfeited their Round 1 offer.

After offers were accepted or declined (starting in Round 1 and continuing after Round 2), CPS began to make offers from the waitlists. Students were given 48 hours to respond to a waitlist offer and remained on waitlists for their higher-ranked programs, even if they accepted an offer. Waitlists were managed by central office rather than individual programs and were to be continually updated through the end of ninth grade.

Options Available to Incoming Ninth-Graders

Students could use GoCPS to complete two applications with the same deadline—one for the SEHS programs and one for all other high school choice programs.

---

5 Fewer than 2 percent of ninth-graders in fall 2018 ultimately enrolled in a special education or alternative high school, based on author calculations using fall 2018 Masterfile data.

6 The new programs are housed at Curie, Foreman, Mather, and Solorio High Schools.

FIGURE 1
GoCPS Application Timeline for Prospective Ninth-Graders

Round 1

Aug 2017	Oct 2017	Dec 2017	Jan/Feb 2018	Mar 2018	Apr 2018
GoCPS Account Activation Families were invited to activate their GoCPS Accounts. Applications were not yet opened, but families were invited to explore their options.	**GoCPS Applications Open** CPS delayed accepting applications by one week to 10/10/17 and pushed back the application deadline accordingly.	**Round 1 Application Deadline** GoCPS online applications were due by 11:59pm on 12/22/17. 5:00pm deadline at OAE for paper applications.	**Schedule Events** Students needed to schedule any admissions screenings such as exams, interviews, information sessions, etc. through GoCPS.	**First Round Offers Extended** On 03/30/18, students were issued offers and waitlist information for each program to which they applied as well as programs for which they had guaranteed enrollment, e.g. neighborhood program or continuing enrollment.	**Deadline to Accept/Decline** 04/13/18 was the deadline for accepting or declining any offer received in Round 1. Students could also accept a neighborhood or other program to which they had guaranteed enrollment.

Students who applied to an SEHS program could rank up to six out of 11 available programs in Round 1, and students who applied to choice high school programs could rank up to 20 programs among the 273 different options offered for incoming ninth-graders in Round 1. Programs were offered to applicants in Round 2 only if there were seats available after applicants accepted Round 1 offers (**see Figure 2** for information about how seats were distributed by program and school type).

For the SEHS application, students received at most one offer to the highest-ranked program for which they were eligible and seats were available. For the choice high school application, students received a single best offer, based on how they ranked the programs, program eligibility requirements, priority groups, program capacity, and their lottery number or application points. (We explain these components in more detail below.) In addition, students were guaranteed a seat in the general education program at their neighborhood high school, even if they did not rank it on their application. For all students, their neighborhood general education program was among those they could accept when responding to their application offer.

Ultimately, students could have chosen from up to four options:

1. **An offer from a choice high school program** the student ranked on the choice application;

2. **An offer from a SEHS program** the student ranked on the SEHS application;

3. **A guaranteed seat in their neighborhood high school** general education program (applicable to all students who were living in Chicago); and

4. **A guaranteed seat at a continuing enrollment school** where the student was enrolled for eighth grade (e.g., a school that serves students in grades 6-12 or 7-12). Most applicants attended CPS elementary schools that serve grades K-8, so this did not apply for those students.[7]

---

[7] About 4 percent of applicants were enrolled in eighth grade at a school with guaranteed continuing enrollment into ninth grade.

Round 2

Apr 2018

Round 2 Applications Open

On 04/30/18 CPS opened the application period for Round 2. 197 programs were open to applicants including 4 programs not offered in Round 1.

Apr/May 2018

Schedule Events

Students had to attend any required information sessions for Round 2 applications. Students were only eligible to apply to available SEHSs if they had already taken the admissions exam.

May 2018

Round 2 Application Deadline

GoCPS online applications were due on 05/06/18.

June 2018

Round 2 Offers Posted, Response Deadline, Waitlists Open

06/01/18 Students were issued offers and waitlist information for each program to which they applied in Round 2.

06/08/18 Deadline to accept or decline any offer.
06/13/18 Waitlists opened.

July 2018

Transfer Window Opens

On 07/01/18, students could request transfers to programs for which they were eligible and that had available seats.

FIGURE 2
Seats Available by Program and School Type

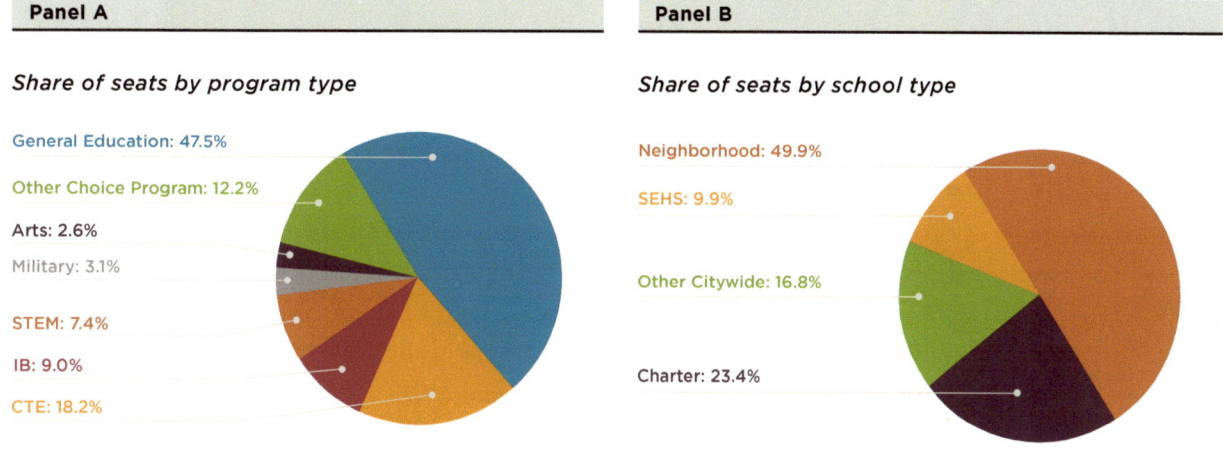

Panel A — *Share of seats by program type*
- General Education: 47.5%
- Other Choice Program: 12.2%
- Arts: 2.6%
- Military: 3.1%
- STEM: 7.4%
- IB: 9.0%
- CTE: 18.2%

Panel B — *Share of seats by school type*
- Neighborhood: 49.9%
- SEHS: 9.9%
- Other Citywide: 16.8%
- Charter: 23.4%

Note: Author calculations from program data for fall 2017 applications for ninth-graders entering high school in fall 2018. Program types categorized as "Other Choice Program" include SEHS, honors, and dual language programs, among others. SEHS school type includes any school that houses a SEHS program. A neighborhood school is any school that houses a neighborhood program. Other citywide schools are schools without an attendance area program that are not charter or selective schools.

The Mechanics Behind Offers: Lotteries and Application Points

For both the choice and SEHS applications, a computerized selection process assigned students to the highest-ranked program on their application for which they were eligible and for which there were available seats. For some choice programs (e.g., IB, military, arts programs), the order of admission was based on application points, so offers were made to the highest-scoring students first. Application points were most commonly constructed from measures on things like test scores, grades, or auditions. However, most choice programs (e.g., CTE programs, charter schools) admitted students at random based on their lottery number.

The process for admitting students to choice programs is called "deferred acceptance," and it has been applied in many different settings. One of the best-known uses is for the assignment of medical residents to hospitals. Deferred acceptance is commonly used because no student loses a seat at a preferred program to a student who is ordered below them in terms of priority group, lottery number, or points. Under this process, students benefited most from ranking programs on their application in the order that they wanted to attend them (i.e., their most preferred program ranked number one). In other words, GoCPS was setup so that there would be no need for applicants to "game the system" when considering how to rank programs.[8]

As in years past, the SEHS program admission criteria included application points based on seventh-grade academic performance and a separate admission exam. Seats at each SEHS were reserved for students living in different neighborhood "tiers," defined by socioeconomic status (SES) measures. Each Census tract was assigned to one of four tiers in order to ensure representation of students from various SES levels at the selective high schools. The process for admitting students to SEHS programs was a special case of deferred acceptance under which students were considered for admission in the order of a single measure, in this case their total application score.

Ultimately, program offers were driven by how many students the program could serve and its pre-designated priorities, such as siblings or students living close to the school.[9] Programs with lotteries admitted students in the order of their randomly assigned lottery number until seats were filled, and programs with application points admitted students in the order of their points until seats were filled. Points-based programs could also have a minimum cutoff score, below which students were not admitted even if seats were available. About 70 percent of the total potential choice seats were randomly assigned via lottery, and the remaining 30 percent were designated to be assigned by application points.

Program Eligibility Requirements and Priority Groups

Program eligibility requirements have continuously been among the most complicated aspects of the high school application process. Programs with eligibility requirements for applications set minimums on one or more academic indicators—NWEA test scores, seventh-grade core GPA, seventh-grade attendance rates. Applicants who did not meet these minimums were prevented from applying to these programs. Some programs had additional admissions requirements, such as attending an information session, submitting a portfolio of work, auditioning, participating in an interview, submitting an essay, and/or submitting recommendation letters. Students applying to these programs had to complete any additional requirements by a specified date in order to be considered for admission. In other words, not meeting one of these additional requirements meant that an applicant was ineligible for admission to that program. Further, some programs that admitted students based on an application score set minimum cutoff scores for admission. This was true for a little over one-half of the programs that admitted students based on points. We provide examples of eligibility requirements for different types of programs, but note that the examples are not exhaustive.

---

8   This property relies on students being allowed to order all of the available programs. GoCPS only allows students to rank up to 20 choice programs and six SEHS programs. Most students were only interested in attending a smaller set of programs, and more than 90 percent of students ranked fewer than 20 programs. As a result, we do not think this constraint on the number of programs an applicant can list is problematic. This is potentially more of an issue with SEHS programs because students can only rank six SEHS programs, and about 15 percent of students listed the maximum number.

9   The number of seats at each program is determined jointly by school principals and central office.

Examples of Eligibility Requirements		
Program	Eligibility Requirements in Order to Apply	Post-Application Eligibility Requirements for Admission
Neighborhood School General Education Programs	No eligibility requirements for students living in the attendance area boundary. There may be minimum requirements for students living outside the boundary.	None
Charter School Programs	No eligibility requirements.	None
Most CTE Programs	No eligibility requirements.	None
IB Programs	Students must have a minimum seventh-grade core GPA of 2.5. General education and 504 plan students are required to have a minimum percentile of 24 on both the reading and math NWEA MAP tests in seventh grade, while students with Individualized Education Plans (IEPs) and English Learner (EL) students are required to a have a minimum combined percentile of 48 in reading and math on the NWEA MAP.	Students must attend an information session to be eligible for admission. Each program sets its own minimum application score for admission.
Military Academy Programs	Students must have a minimum combined NWEA MAP percentile of 48.	Applicants must attend an information session at which students sign a commitment agreement, take an assessment, and write a brief essay. Service learning academies set minimum application scores for admission.
Selective Enrollment High School Programs	General education and 504 plan students must have a minimum percentile of 24 on both the reading and math NWEA MAP tests in seventh grade. Students with IEPs and EL students are required to a have a minimum combined percentile of 48 in reading and math on the NWEA MAP.	The selective enrollment admission exam is required for SEHS admission. Students must achieve an application score of 600 or higher to be eligible for admission.

Many programs also had priority groups that establish the order of admission for students. Priority groups included the following:

- Siblings of current students,
- Students living within the high school attendance area or another geographic boundary,
- Students meeting minimum test score percentiles,
- Students attending specific elementary schools, or
- Students' SES as reflected by CPS's neighborhood tier categorization.

While the GoCPS platform centralized applications under a single system, to a large extent, the eligibility requirements and priority groups were not made consistent across programs. That is, principals still had autonomy over setting admissions requirements. However, some programs had consistent requirements across schools. For example, charter schools were not allowed to have eligibility requirements, but, as with many programs, priority groups did determine the order in which their lotteries were run. In all, we identified 35 unique combinations of application requirements determined by minimum test scores, GPA, and/or attendance rates. That said, only 39 percent of programs had some sort of application requirement.

In this chapter, we intend to provide an overview of the GoCPS applications and admission process. There are many more details available on the GoCPS website[10] and in our previously released preliminary study.[11] We now turn to present findings regarding applications and offers, as well as ninth-grade enrollment.

---

[10] Chicago Public Schools (n.d.).

[11] Barrow, Sartain, & de la Torre (2018).

CHAPTER 2

GoCPS Applications & Offers

Key Takeaways on Applications and Offers

- In fall 2017, almost all CPS eighth-graders used GoCPS to apply to high school. The average applicant applied to about seven choice programs, though they could have listed up to 20 choice programs.
  - Programs varied in their application rates with arts programs, CTE programs, and programs at schools with high accountability ratings in high demand.
  - Students living in the lowest SES (Tier 1) neighborhoods and Black students applied to more programs, on average, but were less likely than other students to list a school with a high accountability rating at the top of their application.
- Four of every five applicants received an offer from a top-three program they applied to, and about one-half from their top program.
- Students living in Tier 1 neighborhoods and Black students were the most likely to receive an offer from a top-three program they applied to compared to other students.
- Almost one in three applicants did not complete at least one choice program admission requirement after submitting an application and were thus made ineligible to receive an offer. Black and Latino students were less likely to complete these requirements compared to students of other races/ethnicities.
- Offers were made to applicants as described on the GoCPS website. Lotteries were random, and programs with points-based admission offered seats to the highest-scoring eligible applicants first.

Eighth-graders in the fall of 2017 were the first group of students to use GoCPS to apply to high school. In August 2018, the UChicago Consortium and the Federal Reserve Bank of Chicago released a preliminary study, which provided a comprehensive examination of the applications to Choice programs and the offers the district made to students.[12] We summarize the main findings in this chapter.

Engagement with GoCPS was High

Overall, we found that about 24,000 CPS eighth-graders, as well as over 2,000 students from outside the district, submitted an application using GoCPS in either Round 1 or Round 2. **Table 1** provides a breakdown of the number of applicants and non-applicants.

Compared to applicants, non-applicants who were enrolled in CPS in eighth grade were less likely to qualify for free/reduced-price lunch and more likely to be White. Non-applicants were also more likely to have an IEP than applicants. Part of this latter difference may be because some IEP students were assigned to special education cluster programs outside of the GoCPS system.

TABLE 1
Almost All CPS Eighth-Graders Completed a High School Application using GoCPS

Number of Students	Action Taken
26,819	Applied to Any High School Program using GoCPS
24,142	Were Enrolled in CPS
2,677	Were from Outside of CPS
2,177	CPS Eighth-Graders DID NOT Apply

Note: Includes applications in either Round 1 or Round 2. We calculated these numbers using CPS fall enrollment Masterfiles as of October 2, 2017 and October 1, 2018. Applicants who were currently enrolled in CPS in fall 2017 had to be enrolled in eighth grade and not enrolled in a special education dual enrollment program or a specialized alternative school. We further dropped any active CPS student in the 2018 fall Masterfile who was enrolled in a grade other than ninth or enrolled in a special education dual enrollment program or specialized alternative school.

---

12 Barrow et al. (2018).

On average, applicants ranked about seven choice programs and two SEHS programs in the first application round. White students and students from high-SES neighborhoods (Tier 4) applied to fewer programs than other subgroups.

While applicants could rank up to 20 programs on the choice application, applicants ranked 7.4 choice programs, on average. Only 5 percent of applicants ranked 20 programs, about one-half of applicants ranked between one and six programs, and 5 percent ranked no choice programs. On average, students ranked 2.4 SEHS programs with 38 percent ranking no SEHS programs and 15 percent ranking the maximum of six programs. **Figure 3** shows the average number of choice and SEHS programs ranked for different student subgroups in Round 1. (**Table A.1 in the Appendix** shows the correlation between race/ethnicity and neighborhood tier.)

In the preliminary report released in 2018, we found that White students and students who lived in higher-income neighborhoods typically ranked fewer programs than students of other races/ethnicities or students who lived in less affluent neighborhoods. Students from outside of CPS tended to apply to fewer choice programs but more SEHS programs than students already enrolled in CPS. These differences are potentially important because they relate to an applicant's likelihood of receiving an offer. Specifically, a student's probability of receiving an offer at a choice program was higher if they applied to more programs.[13]

Most students applied to at least one program at a school with a high accountability rating, though students living in Tier 1 neighborhoods and Black students were the least likely to list one of these programs at the top of their application.

A key goal for CPS is that all students receive a high-quality education. The district defines school quality using their school accountability system, SQRP (School Quality Rating Policy). While there are shortcomings to using this metric **(see the box titled *CPS's School Accountability System: SQRP*** for more information on construction and limitations), including the fact that students and families may seek out schools that provide programming or features not accounted for in SQRP. We include it in our analysis to be consistent with district policy.

FIGURE 3

Number of Programs Ranked Differed by Student Neighborhood SES and Race/Ethnicity

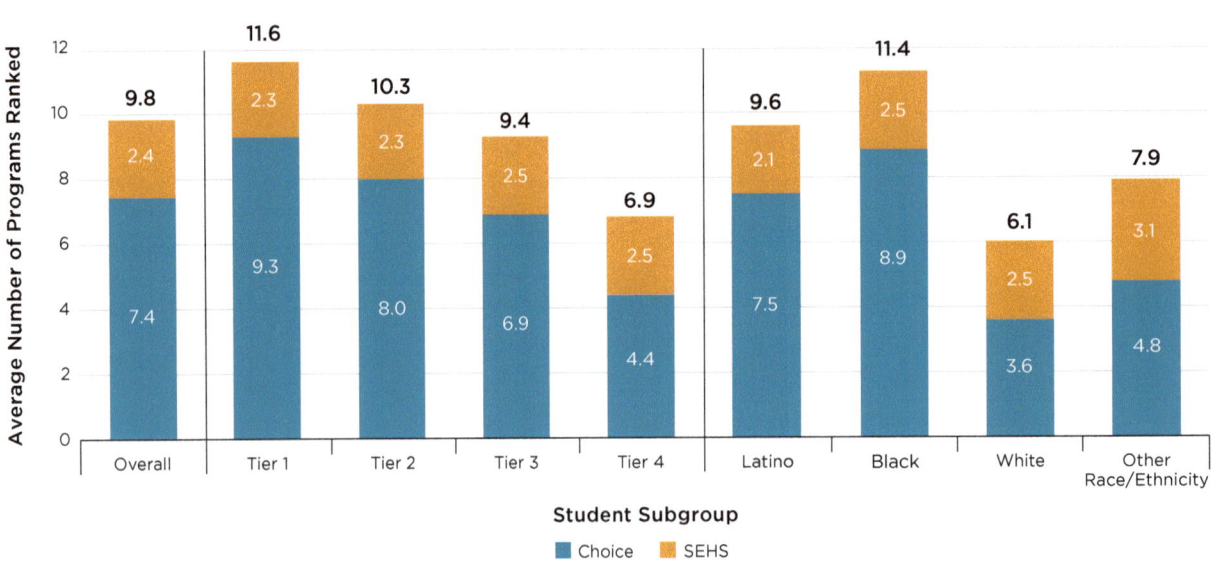

Average number of choice and SEHS programs ranked by student subgroup

Note: The number of programs ranked reflected in this figure includes choice and SEHS programs. Tier 1 Census tracts are relatively low-SES neighborhoods, while Tier 4 Census tracts are relatively high-SES neighborhoods. The "Other" race/ethnicity category includes Asian students, multi-race/ethnicity students, and students who are missing race/ethnicity information, which is disproportionately true for applicants not enrolled in CPS for eighth grade.

---

[13] Barrow et al. (2018).

CPS's School Accountability System: SQRP

CPS has a goal of ensuring that all students receive a high-quality education. In the district's Annual Regional Analysis (ARA) planning document, "high-quality" is defined as a seat at a school with top accountability ratings (SQRP Level 1+ or 1). The ARA divides the district into geographic regions and provides an accounting of how the schools in each region perform on the accountability system as well as programmatic offerings at the schools. In addition, the ARA shows the number of open seats in each school accountability level overall and by region of the city.

Over the past few years, the district has been raising awareness about school accountability ratings and working to get students across the city into seats at schools with high levels of performance. Families and students can access information about SQRP through the CPS website, and applicants can sort schools based on their accountability ratings in the GoCPS platform. Locally, schools also advertise their SQRP level of performance on marquees and banners.

SQRP ratings are released each fall using the prior year's school outcome data. For high schools, the SQRP is based on a number of indicators, including student performance levels and growth on standardized tests, Freshman OnTrack rates, graduation rates, and college enrollment and persistence rates. The ratings also incorporate school climate measures based on survey reports by students and teachers. The rating categories range from Level 1+ (the highest) to Level 3 (the lowest). We note, though, that a school's SQRP rating can change from one year to the next. Thus, the school may not have the same rating in the year the student enrolls as it did when students and families were selecting schools. In addition, SQRP is currently about an entire school's performance level, whereas students apply to specific programs in schools via GoCPS. A school with a low accountability rating may have a specialized program that attracts a number of students, and the SQRP may not reflect the quality of that specific program.[B]

Measuring school quality is challenging. School accountability ratings include metrics that reflect the school's contribution to student learning and improvement as well as family background and SES. The data that comprise the SQRP ratings depend on indicators that often represent a combination of students' prior backgrounds and family and community resources in addition to how a school contributes to student success. For example, the level of student test scores is highly correlated with prior educational experiences, while a growth metric may reflect more about what a school does to support learning. Both the student body composition in terms of peers and school quality likely matter to families as they consider high school choices. We rely on SQRP ratings in our analyses as a measure of school quality in order to be consistent with the ways in which the district is considering school quality and the different options that are available to students.[C]

[B] The majority of schools (57 percent) have only a single program with another 25 percent having 2-3 programs.

[C] For more information on SQRP, see the district's website: https://cps.edu/Performance/Pages/PerformancePolicy.aspx?nt=1.

We find that Black students and Tier 1 students were less likely than other students to rank a program located at a school with a high accountability rating (SQRP Level 1+/1) at the top of their application (**see Figure 4**). Specifically, 60 percent of Black applicants listed a program at a high accountability school at the top of their application, compared with 82 percent of Latino applicants and 94 percent of White applicants. Additionally, about two of every three applicants living in Tier 1 neighborhoods (66 percent) ranked a Level 1+/1 school at the top, compared with 90 percent of applicants living in Tier 4 neighborhoods.

We note that our data cannot answer questions about why these patterns exist. Additionally, because application data were not collected centrally in years prior to GoCPS, we cannot compare these patterns to earlier cohorts of eighth-graders. However, the GoCPS application data provide information for policymakers, families, and community members to use in conversations about access to different kinds of schools, as well as about what characteristics students and families most value in selecting a high school program.

Figure 4

The Percent of Students Who Ranked a Highly Rated School Differed by Neighborhood SES and Race/Ethnicity

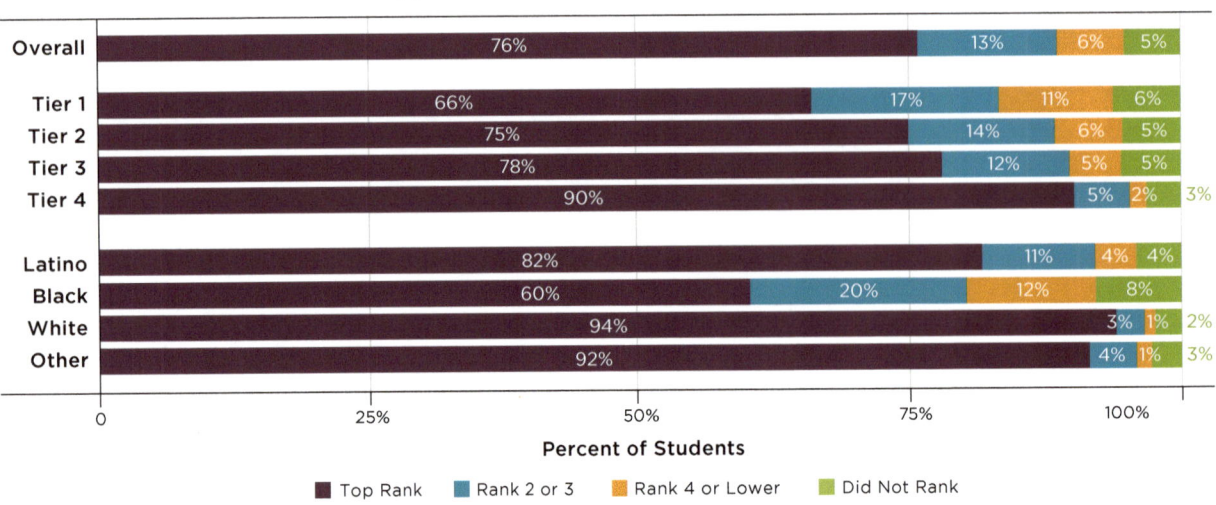

Student applications to level 1+/1 schools by student subgroup

Note: The applications in this figure include only choice programs, and reflect the highest ranking given to a program at a highly rated school. We assigned each program to have the SQRP level of the school in which the program was located. SQRP is calculated at the school level. Tier 1 Census tracts are relatively low-SES neighborhoods, while Tier 4 Census tracts are relatively high-SES neighborhoods. The "Other" race/ethnicity category includes Asian students, multi-race/ethnicity students, and students who are missing race/ethnicity information, which is disproportionately true for applicants not enrolled in CPS for eighth grade. Percentages may not add up to 100 due to rounding. Data and methods are described in the Appendix.

Application rates varied across programs: Arts and CTE programs, as well as SEHS programs and programs at schools with high accountability ratings, were likely to be ranked highly on applications.

Information about application rates for choice programs was unavailable prior to the adoption of GoCPS, as data and reporting were not centralized. With the single GoCPS application system, CPS-wide application rates for specific programs and schools have become available for the first time. With nearly 300 programs to choose from, patterns emerged in terms of more and less popular programs. In **Figure 5**, we show how many students applied to each program, as well as whether the student ranked the program first (shown in purple), second or third (blue), or fourth or lower (yellow). Each bar represents a single program, and the height of each bar represents the total number of applicants who ranked the program at any level on their application. There is a lot of variation in terms of program application rates, with some programs yielding applications in the 1000s and others with fewer than 100 applications.

Out of 284 programs offered, 61 (21 percent) had more than 10 times as many applications as seats available. Arts, CTE, and SEHS programs; programs basing admissions on points; and programs in schools highly rated on the district's SQRP measure were more likely to be in high demand. Notably, many of the high-demand programs (roughly 50 percent) were relatively small programs with fewer than 50 seats available. These programs tended to be arts and CTE programs. High-demand arts programs averaged 20 applications per seat, while CTE programs averaged nearly 30 applications per seat. The largest of the high-demand programs tended to be the SEHSs that had anywhere from 100 to 1000 seats available and averaged 21 applications per seat.

On the other end of the spectrum, 22 programs (8 percent) had fewer applications than seats available. General education and military programs and programs located in schools with low SQRP ratings were more likely to be in low demand. These programs were typically larger programs than those on the high-demand list, and one program was located in a high school with high-demand programs, as well.

We note that information on program demand, based on how often programs are listed on applications alone, is incomplete because all students were entitled to enroll in their neighborhood school's general education program, even if they did not rank the program on their application. In addition, students who were enrolled in

FIGURE 5
Program Application Rates Varied Widely

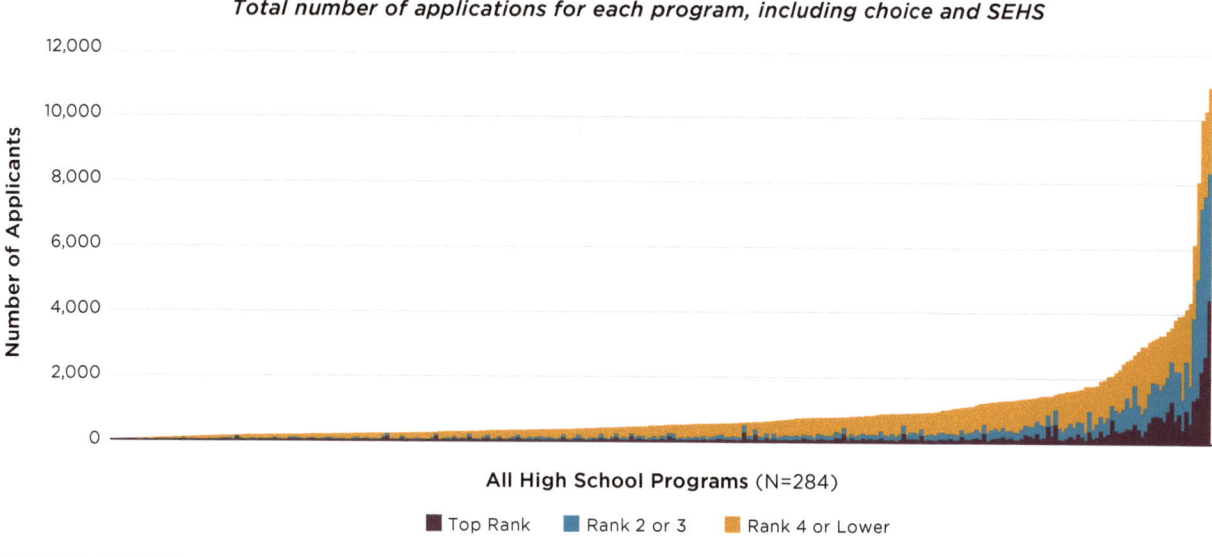

Note: Each bar represents a high school program to which students could apply. Applications to both SEHS and choice programs are represented in the figure.

a program in eighth grade that also served high school grades (e.g., an academic center or a charter school) were eligible to continue in that program without having to apply. Another complicating factor is that students could submit applications to multiple programs, but ultimately could only receive one offer and enroll in one seat. Listing a program high on an application increased a student's odds of receiving an offer. There were some programs that were listed often on applications, but students typically did not rank them highly. This could mean that a program appearing to be in high demand in terms of applications, may actually have made few offers because it was not often listed near the top of applications.

Almost all applicants received an offer, and about one-half received an offer from their top-ranked program. Almost all applicants from Round 1 (93 percent) received an offer at a program they ranked on their application. For 51 percent of applicants, the offer was for their top-ranked program; 81 percent received an offer from one of their top-three ranked programs. Of the 7 percent who did not receive an offer, about one-fourth submitted an application in Round 2, and many were waitlisted for programs they applied to in Round 1. At the end of Round 2, 94 percent of choice applicants had been offered a seat at one of the programs to which they applied. Students who did not receive an offer in either round tended to rank fewer programs, were more likely to live in Tier 4 neighborhoods, and had higher GPAs and average test scores (see Table A.2 in the Appendix).

An applicant's likelihood of receiving an offer from a program they ranked at the top was higher if that program had fewer applications relative to seats available. Students from the lowest-SES neighborhoods (Tier 1) were the most likely to be offered one of their top-three ranked programs (83 percent). Among the race/ethnicity subgroups, Black students were the most likely to be offered one of their top-three ranked programs (86 percent). Students in the "Other" race/ethnicity subgroup, which included Asian students, multi-race/ethnicity students, and students with missing race/ethnicity information, were the least likely to be offered a top-three ranked program and the most likely not to have an offer at the end of both application rounds. This is in part because students in this group were more likely to apply to programs that were in the highest demand. **Table 2** shows offer status overall and by student neighborhood tier and race/ethnicity subgroups. The first three columns are restricted to Round 1 offers, whereas the last column shows offer status at the end of both rounds.

TABLE 2

Most Choice Applicants Are Offered a Seat at One of Their Top-Ranked Programs

Choice Program Offer Status Overall and by Student Neighborhood Tier and Race/Ethnicity				
Student Subgroup	Number of Applicants (in R1)	Offered Top-Ranked Choice Program (in R1)	Offered Seat at Top 3 Ranked Choice Program (in R1)	Offered Any Choice Seat (in R1 or R2)
Overall	25,238	51%	81%	94%
Neighborhood Tier				
Tier 1	7,107	52%	83%	97%
Tier 2	7,161	49%	81%	96%
Tier 3	6,541	50%	79%	94%
Tier 4	4,429	55%	80%	90%
Race/Ethnicity				
Latino	12,230	47%	78%	95%
Black	8,940	56%	86%	97%
White	2,238	56%	80%	89%
Other	1,830	47%	75%	88%

Note: About 400 choice applicants who only participated in Round 2 are included only in the final column. Not shown are the roughly 1,200 applicants who only completed a SEHS application. The "Other" race/ethnicity category includes Asian students, multi-race/ethnicity students, and students who are missing race/ethnicity information, which is disproportionately true for applicants not enrolled in CPS for eighth grade. Tiers 1 through 4 refer to the CPS neighborhood SES categories with Tier 1 being the lowest-SES Census tracts and Tier 4 being the highest-SES Census tracts.

Almost one-third of applicants did not complete choice program admission requirements, such as auditions or information sessions, after submitting an application.

Some program eligibility requirements, such as minimum test score percentiles and GPAs, prevented students from applying to programs for which they were not eligible. Other program eligibility requirements, such as attending an IB information session or completing an audition, had to be completed after submitting an application. This section focuses on applicants becoming ineligible for a program because they did not complete an additional, post-application admissions requirement.[14]

More than one-half of applicants (52 percent) applied to at least one choice program with additional application requirements, and 54 percent of them did not complete at least one of these requirements (see **Table 3**). Even among students whose top-ranked choice program had an additional application requirement, 27 percent did not complete the requirement. There were differential patterns of post-application requirement completion by student SES and race/ethnicity (also shown in **Table 3**). For instance, students living in Tier 4 neighborhoods were most likely to apply to programs with post-application requirements, and they were also most likely to complete those requirements (conditional on applying). However, about half of students living in Tier 1 neighborhoods (48 percent) applied to a program with post-application requirements. Of those students, nearly two in three (64 percent) did not complete at least one screen. We see a similar pattern by student race/ethnicity. For example, conditional on applying

---

[14] Our data are somewhat incomplete in terms of indicators for completing post-application eligibility requirements. For points-based admissions programs that award points for a post-application requirement like an audition or interview, we infer that the applicant did not complete the requirement if they are missing points for that component. For IB applications, we assume that any student who scored above the cutoff score but was deemed ineligible for admission did not attend an IB information session. Finally, because students only had to attend one IB information session, we assume that if the data indicate that the student attended an information session for one IB application, the student met that requirement for all IB applications.

TABLE 3

Students Living in Tier 1 Neighborhoods and Black Students Were Less Likely than Other Students to Complete Post-Application Requirements

Post-Application Requirement Application and Completion Rates by Student Neighborhood Tier and Race/Ethnicity				
	Choice Program at Any Rank		**Top-Ranked Choice Program**	
Student Subgroup	At Least One Choice Program with Post-Application Screens	Did Not Complete at Least One Screen, Conditional On Applying	Program had a Post-Application Screen	Did Not Complete the Screen, Conditional On Applying
Overall	52%	54%	23%	27%
Neighborhood Tier				
Tier 1	48%	64%	17%	37%
Tier 2	49%	57%	20%	30%
Tier 3	52%	53%	23%	26%
Tier 4	61%	37%	37%	17%
Race/Ethnicity				
Latino	53%	52%	24%	25%
Black	44%	71%	14%	47%
White	67%	30%	47%	12%
Other	63%	37%	36%	17%

Note: This table only includes applications to choice programs. The most common programs with post-applications requirements were IB, military, and arts. The Tier 1 Census tracts are relatively low-SES neighborhoods, while Tier 4 Census tracts are relatively high-SES neighborhoods. The "Other" race/ethnicity category includes Asian students, multi-race/ethnicity students, and students who are missing race/ethnicity information, which is disproportionately true for applicants not enrolled in CPS for eighth grade.

to programs with screens, over half (52 percent) Latino students and nearly three in four (71 percent) Black students did not complete at least one screen, making them ineligible for an offer at that program.

We note that most of the missed post-application screens (42 percent) were for IB programs (see Figure 6). In fact, 31 percent of applications to IB programs were incomplete because students did not attend an information session. Though there were fewer seats at (and applications to) military and arts programs, students were even less likely to complete admission requirements at the military high schools and arts programs—roughly two out of three applications (65 percent and 70 percent, respectively) to one of these types of programs were missing an admission requirement.

For IB programs, attending an information session after applying was required for admission, but the information session had no impact on a student's application score. We looked at how many students were eligible for admission to a particular IB program based on their application score, but who were not considered for admission because they did not attend an information session. Here, we found that one-third of applicants to IB programs who scored above the cutoff, and therefore

FIGURE 6

Almost Half of Incomplete Applications Were for IB Programs

Missed post-application screens by program type
(N=14,734)

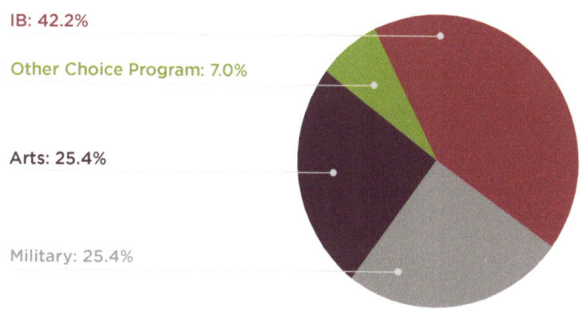

IB: 42.2%
Other Choice Program: 7.0%
Arts: 25.4%
Military: 25.4%

Note: This figure reflects the 14,734 applications to choice programs with post-application requirements that were not completed. Individual applicants (N=7,069) may be included in this figure multiple times if they applied to and did not complete post-application requirements at multiple programs. Programs categorized as "Other" are Kelly HS–AVID, Kelvyn Park HS for students outside the attendance area, and Von Steuben HS–Scholars.

could have been offered a seat, were ineligible to be admitted because they did not attend an information session. This scenario occurred most frequently among Black students and students from low-SES neighborhoods—54 percent of Black students and 41 percent of students from Tier 1 neighborhoods who scored high enough to be admitted to an IB program were ineligible because they did not attend an information session.

The available data cannot explain why applicants did not complete admission requirements, and the high rates of non-completion may reflect that students changed their minds about preferred programs after applications were submitted. However, these rates could also mean that the post-application admission screens and requirements were barriers to students' enrollment in particular types of programs. It is especially concerning that these post-application admission requirements may have created inequity in access to certain types of programs, suggesting there might be room for changes to these requirements. For example, if the purpose of the IB information session is for students and families to get a full understanding of the rigor of the programs, there may be more effective ways to transmit the information, such as an online format, which students could complete at home or at school. Additionally, the district could adopt more supports for ensuring applicants sign up for auditions or information sessions and provide reminders of those dates.

Offers were made to applicants as described on the GoCPS website

The GoCPS website provided detailed information about the process for matching applicants to programs.[15] We conducted an analysis of the selection and offer process in order to verify that offers were made as described on the GoCPS website. Specifically, we asked: Were lottery numbers randomly assigned? Were offers to lottery programs unrelated to applicant characteristics? With programs that admitted students on a points system, did applicants with higher points receive offers before applicants with lower points? Were priority groups, such as sibling preference, honored?

We found that applicants were offered seats according to the process described on the GoCPS website.

- **Programs with Lottery-Based Admission:** Both the assigned lottery number and whether a student was offered a seat were random for students participating in the lottery. This means that student characteristics, including demographics and prior academic achievement, and the order in which students ranked a program on their application were unrelated to how high or low their lottery number was. For example, Black students were not assigned higher (or lower) lottery numbers than Latino students. Therefore, no particular student characteristic, like being female, Latino, or from a high-SES neighborhood, provided undue advantage in the lottery admission process.

- **Programs with Points-Based Admission:** In programs that used application scores (i.e., test scores, audition scores) to determine admissions, students were offered seats in order of application score. Among eligible students who applied to points-based selection programs, no admitted student had a lower application score than a non-admitted student within their priority group. (Students who did not complete post-application requirements were not eligible to be admitted to the program.)

- **Across Lottery and Points-Based Admission Programs:** Priority groups worked as described.[16]

---

[15] Chicago Public Schools (n.d).

[16] For more details about how we validated the assignment mechanism, see pp. 23-27 in Barrow et al. (2018).

CHAPTER 3

Where Did Ninth-Graders Enroll?

Key Takeaways on Student Enrollment

- Most GoCPS applicants accepted an offer through GoCPS.
- Most GoCPS applicants enrolled in the school where they accepted their offer.
- Most CPS eighth-graders who did not use GoCPS either enrolled in a school where they had a guaranteed seat (like their neighborhood school) or left the district.

In our prior report, we found that CPS students used GoCPS to apply to high school at high rates and that offers were made to students as described on the GoCPS website.[17] However, questions remained about where students would ultimately enroll in high schools. First, students did not have to apply to schools for which they had a guaranteed seat (e.g., the general education program at their own neighborhood high school or their current school if it enrolled both middle and high school grades). Further, students had the option of leaving the district for another district or private school.

In this chapter, we show where the entering ninth-grade students enrolled in high school. Many of these students used GoCPS to apply to high school, so we followed those students to see if they enrolled in the schools corresponding to where they accepted program offers. A smaller group of ninth-graders did not apply to high school using GoCPS, and we also provide data on where they enrolled. Finally, we also compare student enrollment in different types of schools before and after the introduction of GoCPS.

Most students who received an offer accepted an offer through GoCPS. Applicants who received an offer, but did not accept an offer, were more likely to be Black, male, or have lower test scores. One of the potential benefits of using a centralized enrollment system like GoCPS is that districts and schools should be able to better project which students will enroll at which schools. At the end of each application round, applicants accepted or rejected their program offer(s). The district could then use the students' selections to plan for enrollment on a school-by-school basis, potentially providing more accurate information to high schools about their incoming ninth-grade class. However, there was some uncertainty about whether or not students who accepted an offer at a specific program would actually enroll in that school, particularly because this was the first cohort to use GoCPS to apply to high school. Other limitations included:

- Not all incoming ninth-graders applied to high school using GoCPS. Students who did not apply could always enroll in their assigned neighborhood high school's general education program or in a continuing enrollment school that they were attending for eighth grade.

- Of the many eighth-graders who used GoCPS to apply to high school and received offers, 16 percent of applicants did not accept an initial offer via the online platform, raising questions about if and where they would ultimately enroll. Students who did not accept an offer were more likely to be Black, male, or have lower test scores.

- About 15 percent of Round 1 applicants participated in Round 2, adding another layer of uncertainty to the breakdown of student enrollment.

---

17 Barrow et al. (2018).

Now, we turn to describing the enrollment choices made by all Round 1 applicants. Overall, 61 percent of applicants enrolled in the school corresponding to the program they accepted. Sixteen percent enrolled at a choice program school where they had not accepted an initial offer; 8 percent enrolled in their neighborhood school; and 13 percent did not enroll in CPS (**see Figure 7**).[18] We note that applicants were placed on waitlists at programs they ranked higher than the program they were offered and at which they were eligible for admission. Offers were made from the waitlists and could explain why students enrolled in a choice program where they had not originally accepted an offer.

Figure 8 shows where applicants enrolled based on their initial offer and response. (**Table A.2 in the Appendix** shows the student characteristics of the different groups represented by Figure 7 and the four pie charts in Figure 8.) Most applicants accepted a choice or SEHS offer via GoCPS. Among these students, 80 percent enrolled where accepted, 11 percent enrolled in a school corresponding to a different choice program (some having been admitted off of a waitlist), 3 percent enrolled in their neighborhood high school, 1 percent enrolled at a SEHS, and 6 percent did not enroll in CPS (**Figure 8, Panel A**). For those students who accepted an offer to a program other than their initial choice program or SEHS offer, 84 percent enrolled in the program they accepted, 9 percent enrolled in a different choice program, 2 percent enrolled in their neighborhood school, and 6 percent did not enroll in CPS (**Figure 8, Panel B**).

Among students who did not accept an initial offer (about 4,300 applicants or 18 percent of those who received offers), enrollment generally fell into three categories: roughly one-third did not enroll in CPS, a little less than one-third enrolled at their neighborhood high school, and one-third enrolled at a choice program school (**Figure 8, Panel C**). For this last group who ended up enrolled in a choice program, a little over 25 percent had been offered or waitlisted for a program at

FIGURE 7
Most Students Enrolled in the School They Accepted through GoCPS

All round 1 applicants (N=26,519)

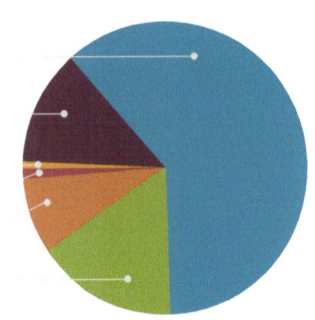

Where Accepted: 61.1%
Did Not Enroll in CPS: 12.8%
Other SEHS: 0.8%
At Continuing: 1.0%
Neighborhood: 8.3%
Other Choice Program: 16.1%

Note: Percentages may not add up to 100 due to rounding. Data and methods are described in the Appendix.

that school in Round 1. Finally, 31 percent of applicants who did not receive an initial offer in Round 1 enrolled at a choice program school; nearly 40 percent did not enroll in CPS; 23 percent ended up at their neighborhood school; and 7 percent enrolled in a continuing program (**Figure 8, Panel D**).

These last two groups of applicants—those who did not accept an offer and those who did not receive an offer—were the most likely to participate in Round 2. Twenty-seven percent of applicants who did not accept an offer participated in Round 2, and 23 percent of applicants who did not receive a Round 1 offer participated in Round 2.

Ultimately, most students who were offered a choice or SEHS seat accepted that offer and enrolled in ninth grade at that school. A few aspects of the GoCPS system meant that some uncertainty about enrollment was to be expected. For example, waitlists moved throughout the spring and summer leading up to ninth grade, so students could have enrolled at a different school if they were admitted off a waitlist. In addition, students could apply for transfers starting in July. Further, the fact that students could enroll at their neighborhood high school or a continuing enrollment school without applying may mean that neighborhood schools have additional uncertainty about ninth-grade enrollment projections.

---

[18] We note that in GoCPS, students applied directly to specific programs located at high schools. Some schools house only a single program, which is the norm at charter schools; other high schools house multiple programs. Given the nature of the enrollment data, we can only verify the high school of enrollment and not the program.

FIGURE 8

Student Enrollment was Largely Consistent with GoCPS Applications and Acceptances

Where GoCPS applicants enrolled in high school by offer and acceptance status

Panel A: 65% of All Applicants

Accepted choice or SEHS offer via GoCPS (N=17,347)

Where Accepted: 79.6%
Did Not Enroll in CPS: 5.9%
Other SEHS: 0.8%
At Continuing: 0.1%
Neighborhood: 2.8%
Other Choice Program: 10.8%

Panel B: 11% of All Applicants

Accepted other programs via GoCPS (N=2,867)

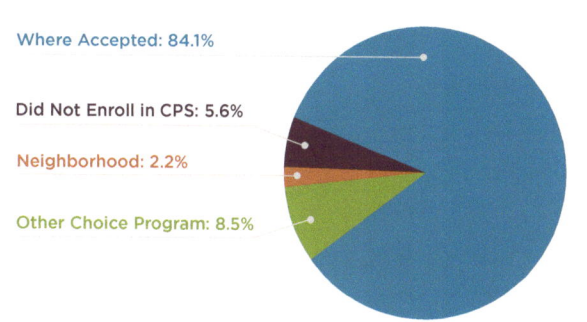

Where Accepted: 84.1%
Did Not Enroll in CPS: 5.6%
Neighborhood: 2.2%
Other Choice Program: 8.5%

Panel C: 16% of All Applicants

Did not accept an initial offer (N=4,264)

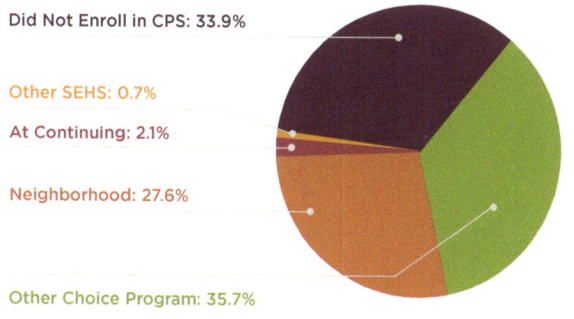

Did Not Enroll in CPS: 33.9%
Other SEHS: 0.7%
At Continuing: 2.1%
Neighborhood: 27.6%
Other Choice Program: 35.7%

Panel D: 8% of All Applicants

Did not receive an initial offer (N=2,041)

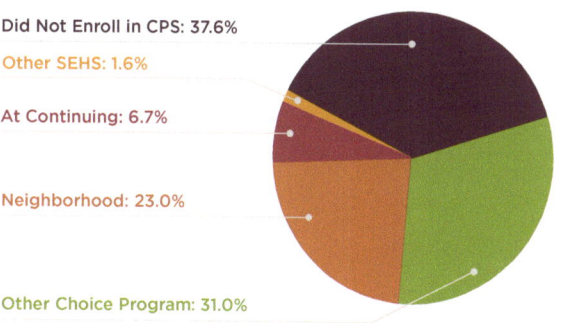

Did Not Enroll in CPS: 37.6%
Other SEHS: 1.6%
At Continuing: 6.7%
Neighborhood: 23.0%
Other Choice Program: 31.0%

Note: Percentages may not add up to 100 due to rounding. Data and methods are described in the Appendix.

CHAPTER 4

The Types of Schools Where Ninth-Graders Enrolled

Key Takeaways on Student Enrollment

- CPS enrolled a similar number of ninth-graders after the introduction of GoCPS as they did in the year prior.
- Student enrollment at different types of schools remained very similar before and after GoCPS. However, there was a small increase in the percentage of students enrolled in neighborhood schools using GoCPS compared to past trends.
- There were no statistically significant changes in the shares of students enrolled in schools with high accountability ratings for all student race/ethnicity and neighborhood tier subgroups. While Black students and students from Tier 1 neighborhoods were less likely to be enrolled in schools with high accountability ratings than other students, these differences existed before the adoption of GoCPS.
- Similarly, there were no statistically significant changes in the average distance traveled to high school overall and by student race/ethnicity groups or neighborhood tier. While differences in average distance to enrolled high school exist across student subgroups, these differences existed before GoCPS.

The implementation of the centralized application process in the fall of 2017 raised questions about whether ninth-grade enrollment would be affected. GoCPS could have made it easier to apply to charter schools in particular. In the past, families had to apply to each charter school or charter management organization individually, whereas GoCPS required only a single application through a centralized platform for all choice programs. This change led to concerns that students who would have otherwise attended neighborhood high schools might now be more likely to apply to and attend charter schools. In this chapter, we investigate whether or not students enrolled in different types of schools at higher or lower rates than in the past, including enrolling in schools with high accountability ratings. Looking at enrollment by accountability rating is important, as the district's goal is to ensure that all students are enrolled in high-quality schools, and the accountability rating system is their proxy for quality. We also look for differences in school enrollment patterns by student neighborhood tier and race/ethnicity.

While we can look at patterns in enrollment by types of schools and student subgroups, we cannot observe the choices that individual students would have made in the absence of GoCPS. It could be the case that aggregate patterns of enrollment were similar to years prior to the implementation of GoCPS, but that individual students would have made different application and enrollment decisions without GoCPS. In addition, it is important to take into consideration that GoCPS has only been in use for one year. Patterns may change after families gain more experience using the system, and as the district and schools make changes to their outreach and programming.

Ninth-grade enrollment numbers were very similar in fall 2018 compared to the years prior to GoCPS. Although overall enrollment in CPS continued to drop between fall 2017 and fall 2018, the number of first-time ninth-graders was relatively unchanged—26,215 first-time ninth-graders enrolled in fall 2018 compared to 26,472 first-time ninth-graders enrolled in fall 2017.[19] The introduction of GoCPS did not correspond with a

---

19 These numbers are slightly lower than those reported for CPS 20th day enrollment because we dropped students who were not enrolled in ninth grade for the first time.

How We Define School Type

For the purposes of the enrollment analysis in this report, we classify schools as being one of five types:

1. **Own Neighborhood:** All students have an assigned high school based on their residential address. In Chicago, these are typically known as "neighborhood" or "attendance area" schools.

2. **Other Neighborhood:** Because of the open enrollment system, students can apply to and enroll in (depending on availability of seats, eligibility, and receipt of an offer) programs at neighborhood schools that are not their own assigned school.

3. **Charter:** These are public schools that are part of the district's portfolio approach to school choice. They are run autonomously, typically by charter management organizations, but they are subject to the district's school accountability system.

4. **Other Citywide:** These high schools do not have attendance area boundaries and are not charter schools. Some examples include magnet schools and military academies.

5. **Selective Enrollment:** Admission to one of these schools is based on academic achievement with additional consideration of the socioeconomic level of the student's home Census tract. Four of these schools also house choice programs, but we classify the school as SEHS.

---

large change in the overall number of first-time ninth-graders enrolling in the district, and the overall number of first-time ninth-graders has been relatively stable since fall 2016.

We also looked at how the percent of ninth-graders enrolled in different types of schools (e.g., neighborhood or charter) changed over time, including after the introduction of GoCPS. **Figure 9** shows ninth-grade enrollment by school type over a five-year period.

In 2018, the distribution of ninth-graders across different types of schools was very similar to the period leading up to the implementation of GoCPS (**see Figure 9**). In fall 2018, 23 percent of ninth-graders enrolled in their assigned neighborhood high school with another 21 percent enrolling in a neighborhood school that was not their default option. Taken together, just under one-half of ninth-graders (44 percent) were enrolled in a neighborhood high school in 2018. This compares to 45 percent of ninth-graders enrolled in a neighborhood high school in the fall of 2014. Enrollment at own neighborhood high school had been declining over the past several years prior to fall 2018. Relative to this declining trend,[20] the small increase in enrollment at own neighborhood high schools in fall 2018 was statistically significant. We emphasize, however, that we cannot conclude that the implementation of GoCPS caused changes in enrollment by school type.

FIGURE 9

Enrollment by School Type was Similar Before and After GoCPS

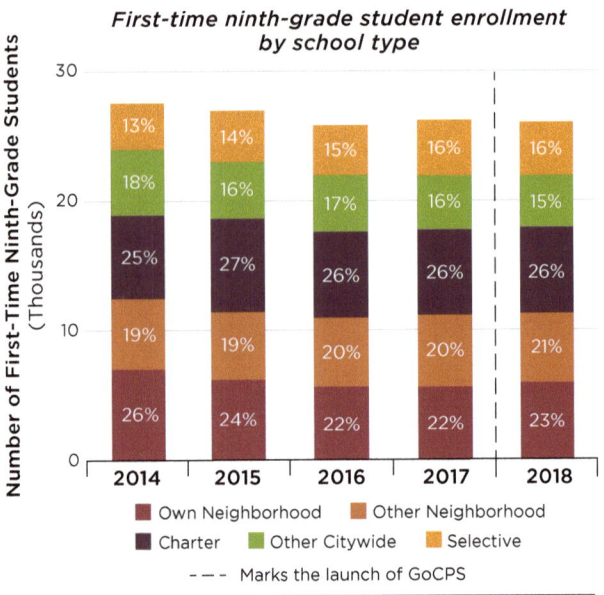

First-time ninth-grade student enrollment by school type

Note: Students represented are restricted to first-time CPS ninth-graders. "Own neighborhood" indicates students attended their assigned neighborhood high school. Percentages may not add up to 100 due to rounding. Data and methods are described in the Appendix.

---

20 In regression models predicting the likelihood of enrolling in a given school type, we included a linear time trend, which goes back to 2014. We then tested whether or not the 2018 enrollment levels deviate from that trend. In other words, the regression estimates allow us to answer the question: Did 2018 enrollment differ from what we would have expected given the prior four years' enrollment? We do this overall, by neighborhood tier, and by race/ethnicity.

Charter school enrollment also remained similar over the period with about one out of every four CPS ninth-grader enrolled in a charter school. The biggest shift was still a relatively small one. In fall 2018, 16 percent of ninth-graders enrolled in a SEHS compared with 13 percent in 2014.[21] Over that same period, there was a corresponding decline in enrollment at other citywide high schools.

Students living in all neighborhood tiers were more likely to attend their neighborhood high school in fall 2018 than in years past. There were no large changes in enrollment by school type for students of different races/ethnicities.

The percent of students enrolled in different types of schools by neighborhood SES (tier) and race/ethnicity also remained relatively stable after the implementation of GoCPS, as shown in **Figures 10 and 11**. These figures are similar to **Figure 9**, but we show just fall 2017 and fall 2018 enrollment patterns. There are clear differences in enrollment across school type by both neighborhood SES and race/ethnicity. Students living in Tier 4 neighborhoods were more likely to enroll in their own neighborhood high school or a SEHS than students living in other tier neighborhoods. However, this was also true in fall 2017 before the implementation of GoCPS.

There were relatively small changes between fall 2017 and fall 2018 within neighborhood tier, although several changes were statistically different from recent trends going back to 2014. For each neighborhood tier, students were slightly more likely to attend their own neighborhood high school than we would have predicted based on recent trends going back to 2014.

By student race/ethnicity, there were also differences in enrollment by school type. Black students were the most likely to be enrolled in charter schools, whereas students of other race/ethnicity groups were more likely to be enrolled in a neighborhood school. Again, these differences existed prior to the use of GoCPS. Within student racial/ethnic groups, we find that both

FIGURE 10

Neighborhood School Enrollment Increased Slightly across Student Neighborhood Tier after GoCPS

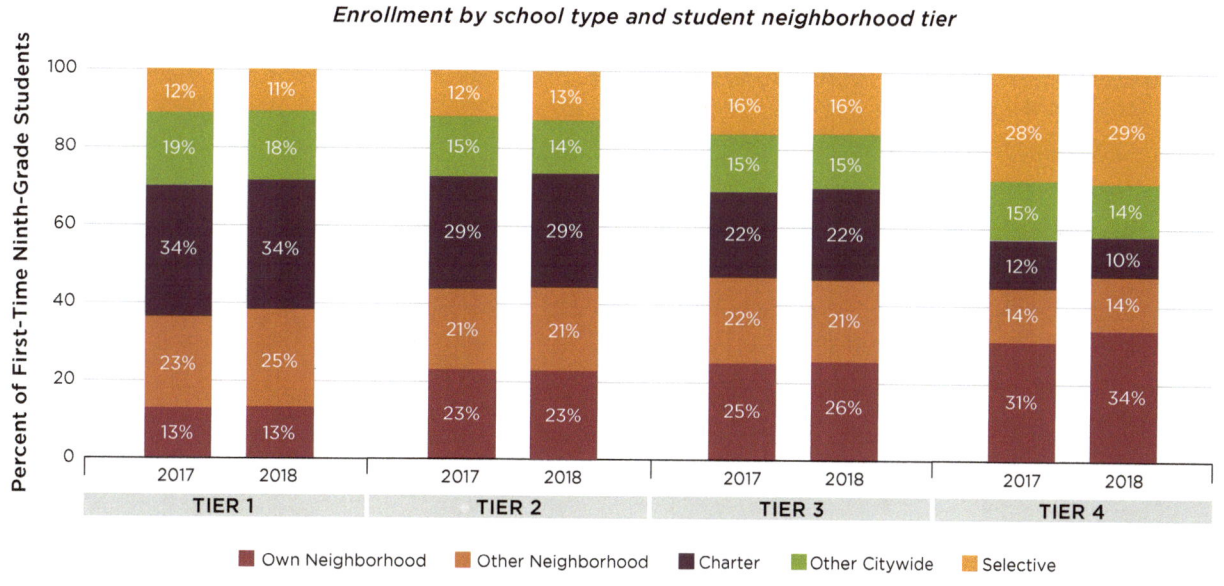

Enrollment by school type and student neighborhood tier

Note: Students represented are restricted to first-time CPS ninth-graders. "Own neighborhood" indicates students attended their assigned neighborhood high school. Tier 1 Census tracts are relatively low-SES neighborhoods, while Tier 4 Census tracts are relatively high-SES neighborhoods. Percentages may not add up to 100 due to rounding. Data and methods are described in the Appendix.

21 This increase could be due to the addition of Hancock High School as a SEHS starting for ninth-graders enrolling in fall 2016 and the completion of an annex to Walter Payton High School, which also increased the number of SEHS seats in fall 2016.

FIGURE 11
Enrollment by Student Race/Ethnicity and School Type was Similar Before and After GoCPS

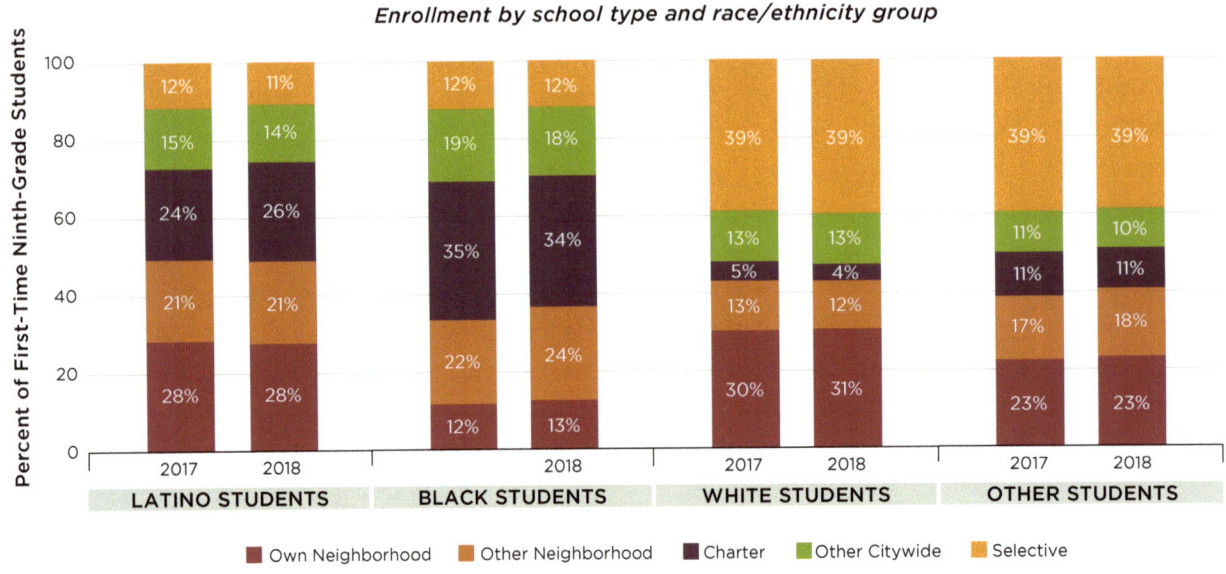

Note: Students represented are restricted to first-time CPS ninth-graders. "Own neighborhood" indicates students attended their assigned neighborhood high school. The "Other" race/ethnicity category includes Asian students, multi-race/ethnicity students, and students who are missing race/ethnicity information, which is disproportionately true for applicants not enrolled in CPS for eighth grade. Percentages may not add up to 100 due to rounding. Data and methods are described in the Appendix.

Black and White students were slightly more likely to attend their own neighborhood school and slightly less likely to attend a SEHS than recent trends would have suggested. Black students were also less likely to enroll in a charter school and White students were less likely to enroll in other citywide schools than in recent trends. However, we note that these changes were small in magnitude, even if statistically significant.

After using GoCPS to apply to high school, student enrollment in schools with high accountability ratings remained similar to previous years.

The share of first-time, ninth-grade students enrolled in high schools with high accountability ratings (SQRP Level 1+/1) was largely unchanged between fall 2017 and fall 2018 (**see Figure 12**). In fall 2018, 65 percent of ninth-grade students were enrolled in a high school with a SQRP rating of Level 1 or Level 1+ compared to 64 percent of ninth-graders in fall 2017 and 62 percent in fall 2016.[22] The share of students enrolled in high

FIGURE 12
Enrollment by School SQRP was Similar Before and After GoCPS

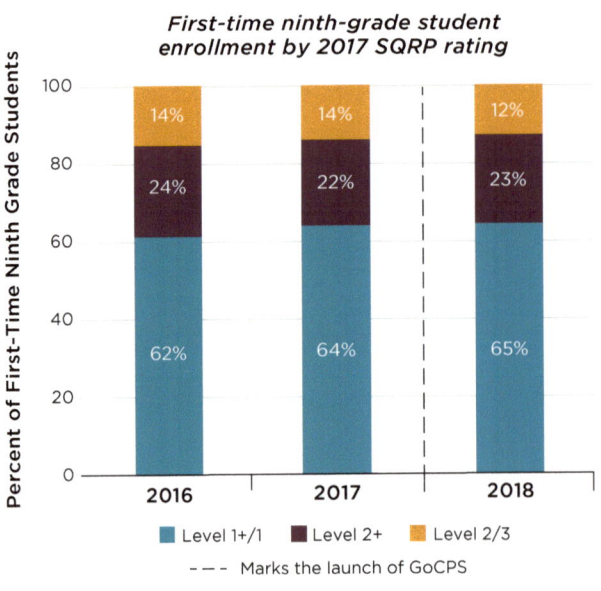

Note: SQRP rating levels were held constant at the 2017 levels to reflect the information available to the first cohort of students and families using GoCPS at the time applications were due. This avoids conflating year-to-year changes in SQRP ratings with changes in student enrollment decisions.

---

[22] Because SQRP ratings change over time, for Figure 12 we hold SQRP ratings fixed at the 2017 levels that were available to the first cohort of students using GoCPS at the time they were making their enrollment decisions. Our conclusion is unchanged if we instead use 2018 SQRP ratings, but the average shares fall because several high schools fell from SQRP Level 1 in 2017 to SQRP Level 2+ in 2018.

schools with low SQRP ratings of Level 2 or Level 3 declined from 14 percent in fall 2017 to 12 percent in fall 2018.

Figures 13 and 14 present shares of students enrolled at schools of different SQRP-level ratings by student neighborhood tier and race/ethnicity group. Across neighborhood tier (**shown in Figure 13**), there were large differences in the shares of students who enrolled in schools with the highest accountability rating levels; over time the changes within groups were relatively small, but students from Tier 4 neighborhoods were a statistically significant 1.5 percentage points more likely to be enrolled in a SQRP Level 1+/1 school in fall 2018 than in fall 2017. There were also large differences across student race/ethnicity groups in the shares of students who enrolled in schools with the highest SQRP rating levels (**see Figure 14**). However, the differences between fall 2017 and fall 2018 were small, and none were statistically significant.

After using GoCPS to apply to high school, students generally traveled similar distances to high school compared to the prior year. However, students living in the lowest-SES neighborhoods, on average, attended a high school farther from their home than they had in previous years.

One potential implication of students attending schools of choice rather than neighborhood schools is an increase in the amount of time students spend traveling to and from school. If GoCPS made it easier for students to attend schools of choice because the costs of applying decreased, one result might be that students spend more time traveling to schools than in the past. However, based on the findings presented previously, we know that a similar percentage of students attended their own neighborhood high school after GoCPS compared to past ninth-grade cohorts. Regardless, we present data on average distance between a student's home and high school.[23]

FIGURE 13

Enrollment in Highly Rated Schools by Student Neighborhood Tier was Similar Before and After GoCPS

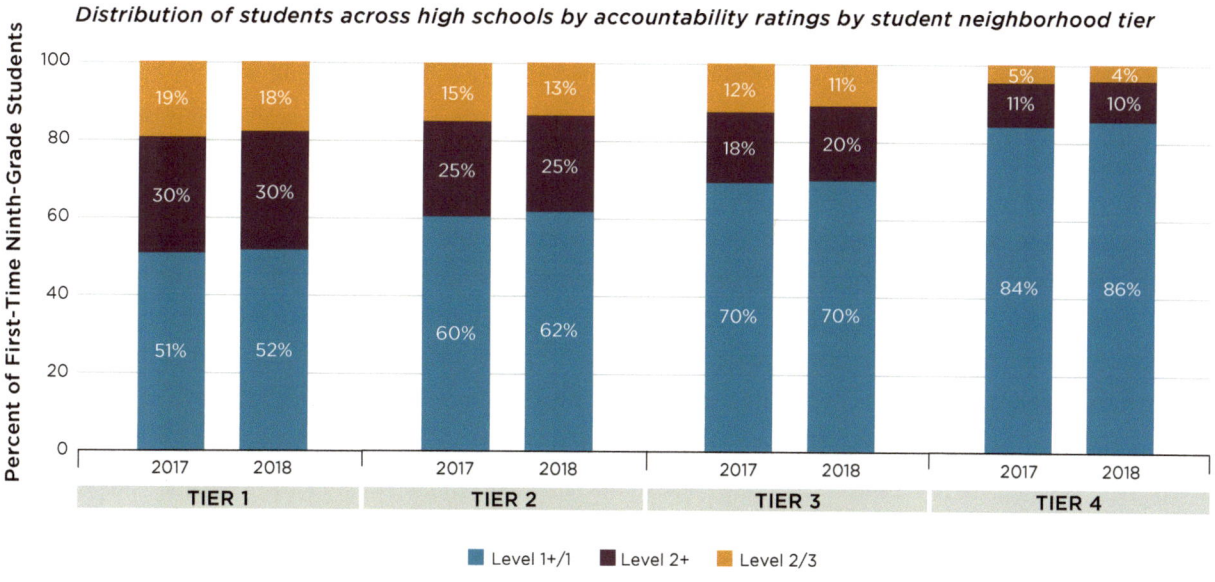

Distribution of students across high schools by accountability ratings by student neighborhood tier

Note: Tier 1 Census tracts are relatively low-SES neighborhoods, while Tier 4 Census tracts are relatively high-SES neighborhoods. SQRP rating levels were held constant at the 2017 levels to reflect the information available to the first cohort of students and families using GoCPS at the time applications were due. This avoids conflating year-to-year change in SQRP with changes in student enrollment decisions. Percentages may not add up to 100 due to rounding. Data and methods are described in the Appendix.

---

23 We use the straight-line distance between a student's home Census block and a high school's Census block.

FIGURE 14
Enrollment in Highly Rated Schools by Student Race/Ethnicity was Similar Before and After GoCPS

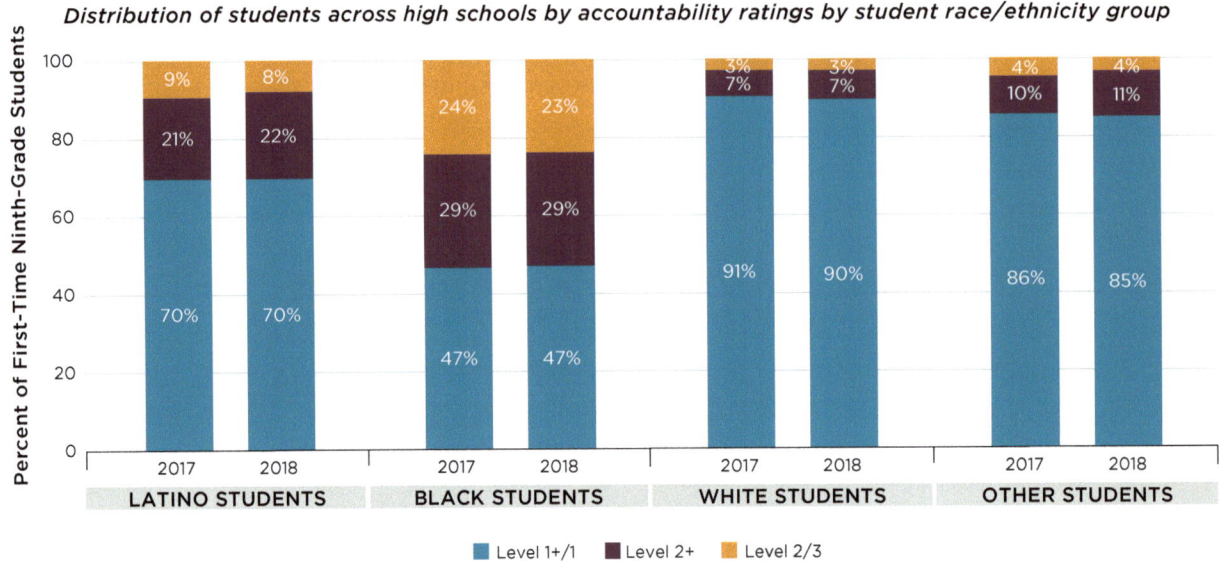

Distribution of students across high schools by accountability ratings by student race/ethnicity group

Note: SQRP rating levels were held constant at the 2017 levels to reflect the information available to the first cohort of students and families using GoCPS at the time applications were due. This avoids conflating year-to-year change in SQRP with changes in student enrollment decisions. The "Other" race/ethnicity category includes Asian students, multi-race/ethnicity students, and students who are missing race/ethnicity information, which is disproportionately true for applicants not enrolled in CPS for eighth grade. Percentages may not add up to 100 due to rounding. Data and methods are described in the Appendix.

Figure 15 shows trends in the average distance traveled over five years by students' neighborhood tier. In 2018, students living in low-SES neighborhoods (Tier 1) traveled 0.11 miles farther to high school than they had in 2017, but this increase is part of a trend that has been occurring over the past several years. Therefore, the 2018 increase in distance traveled for Tier 1 students cannot be attributed to GoCPS. However, it is interesting to note that the average distance traveled across tiers has converged over this five-year period so that students living in different tier neighborhoods are traveling more similar distances on average.

Average distance traveled to high school for ninth-graders of different race/ethnicity groups has also remained relatively stable over this period. **Figure 16** shows the average distance traveled over time separately for Black, Latino, White, and Other race/ethnicity students. For example, in fall 2018 Black students lived about 4.5 miles from their enrolled high school, the same as in the years leading up to GoCPS. On average, Latino students traveled 3.2 miles to school in 2018, which was similar to the prior years. Students in the Other race/ethnicity group traveled somewhat less in 2018 (3.8 miles) compared with 2017 (4.0 miles), and this difference across years was marginally statistically significant.

Overall, we do not find large changes in student enrollment patterns before and after the use of GoCPS for high school applications and enrollment. A similar number of ninth-graders were enrolled in different types of schools (e.g., neighborhood, charter) and schools with different accountability ratings (e.g., Level 1+/1) as in years past. This is generally true for students living in different neighborhood tiers and of different race/ethnicity groups. Similarly, ninth-graders were traveling as far to high school on average in 2018 as the prior year. As families and students learn more about the GoCPS application and enrollment system, these patterns may change. This topic certainly warrants continued investigation particularly given the district's goal of ensuring all students have access to strong schools.

FIGURE 15
Distance Traveled by Student Neighborhood Tier was Similar Before and After GoCPS

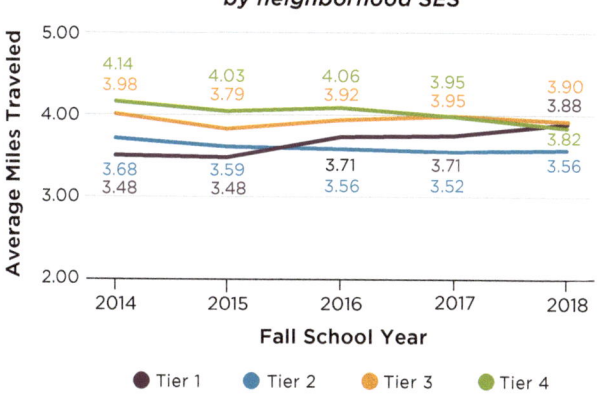

Distanced traveled between home and school by neighborhood SES

Note: CPS assigns Census tracts to SES tier each year. In this analysis, we allowed tracts to change tiers over time to correspond with the CPS tier. Tier 1 Census tracts are relatively low-SES neighborhoods, while Tier 4 Census tracts are relatively high-SES neighborhoods. We use straight-line distance between a student's home Census block and a high school's Census block.

FIGURE 16
Distance Traveled by Student Race/Ethnicity was Similar Before and After GoCPS

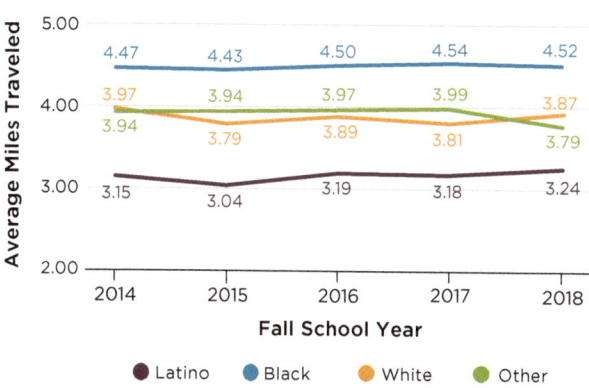

Distanced traveled between home and school by race/ethnicity

Note: We use straight-line distance between a student's home Census block and a high school's Census block. The "Other" race/ethnicity category includes Asian students, multi-race/ethnicity students, and students who are missing race/ethnicity information which is disproportionately true for applicants not enrolled in CPS for eighth grade.

CHAPTER 5

School-by-School Changes in High School Enrollment

Key Takeaways on School-Level Enrollment

- Most high schools enrolled a similar number of ninth-graders in fall 2018 (after GoCPS) compared to fall 2017 (before GoCPS).
- On average, neighborhood high schools experienced small increases in enrollment with correspondingly small declines in other citywide high schools (like military academies) and SEHSs.
- Generally, high schools served similar student populations in terms of demographics and prior achievement before and after the introduction of GoCPS.

The implementation of GoCPS and the resulting centralization of all high school applications to a single platform could have resulted in changes in enrollment levels for individual schools. For example, the centralized information about the programs offered at different high schools could have made families more aware of program options than they had been in the past. GoCPS also meant that students could research specialized programs at neighborhood high schools, for example, which may have attracted students who would not have been aware of those options otherwise. In this chapter, we discuss the evidence on whether and how enrollment changed for schools—both in terms of the number of ninth-graders and the composition of the student body. Specifically, did ninth-grade enrollment numbers change at individual schools? Did the characteristics of the ninth-graders in the school change after GoCPS?

For most schools, the number of ninth-grade students enrolled in fall 2018 was similar to the number enrolled in fall 2017.

For each high school, **Figure 17** shows the number of first-time ninth-grade students enrolled at a given school in 2018 (the vertical axis) compared to 2017 student enrollment (the horizontal axis). Each high school is represented by a circle with the color of the circle representing one of four types of schools—neighborhood, charter, SEHS, or other citywide school.

Schools located on the black diagonal line had the same first-time ninth-grade enrollment in 2017 and 2018. Some natural fluctuations in enrollment are to be expected, but many of the schools represented in the figure were similar in size across the two years.

Another way to summarize changes in school enrollment is to look at the percentage change in enrollment based on 2017 enrollment numbers. We provide that information in **Table 4**. To generate these numbers, we calculated the percentage change in enrollment for each school and then aggregated to the type of school, weighting by the level of enrollment in 2017 so that schools with many students enrolled got more weight

TABLE 4

On Average, Neighborhood and Charter High Schools Experienced Small Increases in Enrollment

Average Change in Ninth-Grade Enrollment between 2017 and 2018 by School Type	
School Type	Average Percent Change in Ninth-Grade Enrollment
Overall	-0.1%
Neighborhood	+3.0%
Charter	+0.1%
Other Citywide	-6.0%
SEHS	-2.3%

Note: The numbers represent the percentage change in first-time, ninth-grade enrollment between 2017 and 2018 weighted by 2017 enrollment. Schools categorized as "Other" are citywide schools that are not charters and do not have attendance area boundaries.

FIGURE 17
School-Level Enrollment Was Generally Stable Between 2017 and 2018

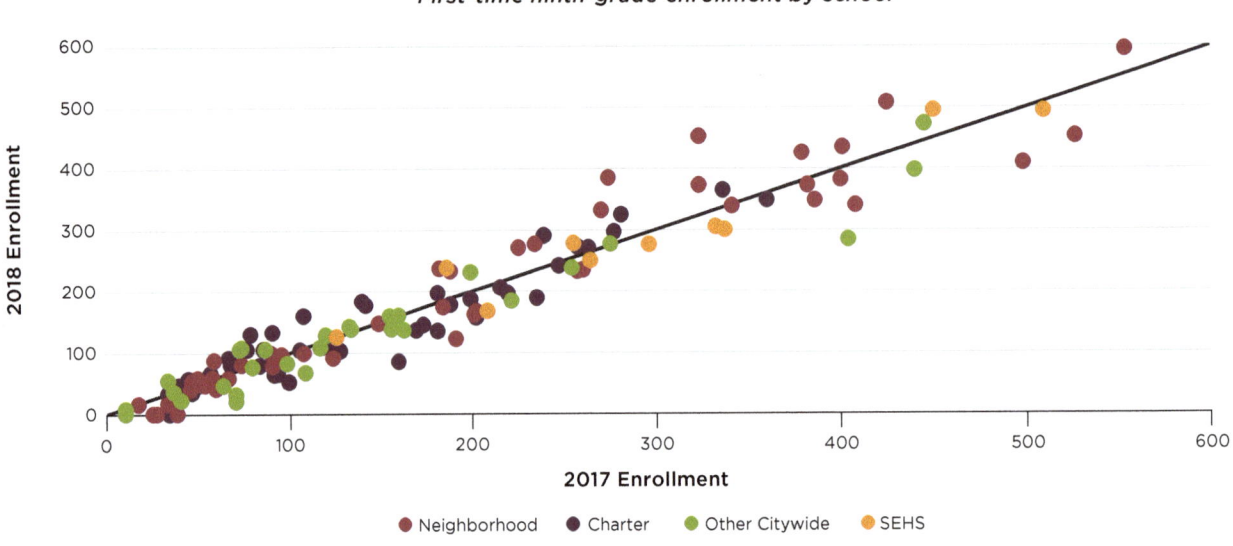

First-time ninth-grade enrollment by school

● Neighborhood ● Charter ● Other Citywide ● SEHS

Note: Enrollment numbers are for first-time ninth-grade students from the fall Masterfile data. Schools categorized as "Other citywide" are schools that are not charters and do not have attendance area boundaries. The correlation between 2017 and 2018 first-time ninth-grade enrollment is 0.98. We excluded schools with first-time ninth-grade enrollment greater than 600 students in order to make the figure easier to read.

than schools with few students enrolled. While overall ninth-grade enrollment declined very slightly, neighborhood school enrollment generally grew between 2017 and 2018, with the typical neighborhood school increasing its ninth-grade population by 3 percent. On the other hand, ninth-grade enrollment at other citywide schools declined by 6 percent on average.

We do not see large changes in the makeup of ninth-grade students served in different types of schools after GoCPS.

While ninth-grade enrollment was relatively stable for most schools between 2017 and 2018, it is possible that GoCPS led to schools attracting applications from different types of students than they had in the past. To that end, we looked at changes in the composition of the ninth-grade student body before and after the use of GoCPS. For example, we examined whether or not charter schools served more or fewer Black or Latino students than in the past, or if neighborhood schools served more or fewer low-achieving or high-achieving students. Ultimately, we did not find big changes in student body composition by school type. We found preliminary evidence that neighborhood schools tended to serve students from a greater number of neighborhoods in the city in 2018 than in 2017. While the change was small, this evidence suggests that GoCPS may have led to a greater dispersion of students to high schools across Chicago, though further research in this area is needed as GoCPS continues to be implemented. This change would be consistent with the notion that applicants may have become more aware of program offerings in other parts of the city via GoCPS.

Overall, there were not large changes in patterns of school-level enrollment with the introduction of GoCPS. Prior to implementation, some parent and advocacy groups raised concerns that certain schools—potentially schools with more experience advertising their programs—might be advantaged by the centralized application system. However, school-level enrollment was generally stable between 2017 and 2018. The first year using GoCPS could have been an anomaly, and these findings might change as students and schools learn more about the system and adapt their behavior in response. With more cohorts of students using GoCPS in the future, we will have a better understanding of whether student enrollment patterns change with the simplified application process.

CHAPTER 6
Interpretive Summary

GoCPS was a big step forward in simplifying the way incoming ninth-grade students applied to and enrolled in high schools. For the first time in the fall of 2017, applications to all high school programs, including charter high schools, were centralized on a common platform with a single deadline.

It is noteworthy that at the time of this report, Chicago was the largest district to have integrated charter schools into a centralized enrollment system. Importantly, applicants received offers from one choice program and potentially one selective enrollment program, rather than, as in previous years, the potential for some students to have received and accepted multiple offers while others received no offers. The switch to GoCPS likely resulted in more certainty for families about where their children would enroll in high school, as well as more certainty for high schools about how many students would likely enroll, and who those students would be.

From this research, we also know that the GoCPS offers were implemented with fidelity. More specifically, students applying to programs that used lottery-based admission appeared to be admitted at random, such that no student subgroups were more or less likely to receive high/low lottery numbers or offers. For non-lottery programs, which admitted students based on applications points, eligible students with higher points were offered seats before students with lower points. Finally, the priority groups described on GoCPS—siblings, for example—were also taken into account. The school assignment algorithm is technically complex, which likely makes the process seem opaque to families, potentially leading them to distrust the system. There may be ways to simplify the system further (e.g., further standardizing admission rules, reducing post-application requirements) in order to reduce application barriers that may create inequities related to student demographic characteristics like race and SES.

CPS students enrolled in ninth grade in ways that were largely consistent with their participation in GoCPS and the program offer they accepted. This likely provided more certainty for schools about ninth-grade enrollment, potentially resulting in schools being better prepared to serve their incoming ninth-grade class. But the design still allows for considerable ambiguity. For example, students could have enrolled in their neighborhood school without applying or accepting an offer. Or, students could have accepted an offer from another program and still enrolled in their neighborhood school. This aspect may have made it difficult for schools, particularly neighborhood schools, to project their ninth-grade enrollment.

At the end of the day, school choice systems are comprised of many policy decisions. GoCPS streamlined the application and enrollment process, but many factors influence where students enroll in high school, and many of those factors are outside the GoCPS system. Policies outside of GoCPS determined where schools and programs were located. Policies outside of GoCPS determined program eligibility and admission criteria and/or priority groups. Policies outside of GoCPS determined how resources were allocated. But all of these policies affect the choices available to students living in different parts of the city and having different academic qualifications.

The centralization of the application process under GoCPS provided new insights about the broad set of choices considered by students and families applying to high school. Before GoCPS, we did not have a comprehensive sense of which public high schools and programs students were applying to. These new data can help district leaders as they manage their diverse set of programs and high schools. In addition, these data allow us to uncover some potential inequities. For instance, we found that Black students were less likely to apply to highly rated schools and were also less likely to complete post-application program requirements than other students. Such findings suggest that some students may face barriers to enrollment in particular types of programs. And, when it came to where students enrolled in the fall, we also saw that Black students were much less likely to be enrolled in a school with a high accountability rating than other students. Although this enrollment pattern existed long before GoCPS, findings like this one raise concerns about how characteristics like a student's race/ethnicity and residential neighborhood influence access to programs and ultimately schooling choices.

What the data from GoCPS and this research do not tell us is why families make the application and enrollment decisions that they do. Students and families made choices based on the information and resources available to them, as well as a deep understanding of their own circumstances and what they value and need in a school. Certainly, some information influencing these choices was not available to us as researchers or even to the district. For example, a school may have particular supports in place that attract and serve families—health clinics, partnerships with non-profit organizations, homelessness services, sports teams, or extracurricular programs—that are not directly reflected in measures like accountability ratings. Students and families may also be concerned about safety while traveling to and from school, transportation costs, crossing gang boundaries, or attending schools unknown to them or their friends and family. These issues should not be minimized. Future research on these considerations, especially as they relate to understanding what families value and what students need to be successful in high school and beyond, is critical. This understanding can help the district, schools, and others develop better supports to help families and students navigate the high school choice process.

Importantly, questions also remain about whether the adoption of a centralized application system results in better matches between students and schools. In the longer term, GoCPS should make it easier for families to find high school options that are a good fit for their children using the streamlined application and enrollment process. This assumption is testable, and we should answer these questions in future research: Did GoCPS ultimately result in fewer student transfers, improved student experiences in high school, and better student educational outcomes? We plan to study these questions as students and the district continue to use GoCPS for high school applications and enrollment and as families continue to learn how to engage with the GoCPS platform. Once questions like these are answered, policymakers will be in a better position to deem the extent to which GoCPS affected students and schools.

References

Barrow, L., & Sartain, L. (2017)
The expansion of high school choice in Chicago Public Schools. *Economic Perspectives, 41*(5), 1-30.

Barrow, L., Sartain, L., & de la Torre, M. (2018)
GoCPS: A first look at applications and offers (Manuscript). Chicago, IL: Federal Reserve Bank of Chicago.

Chicago Public Schools. (n.d.)
About GoCPS. Retrieved from https://go.cps.edu/about-gocps

Appendix

CPS categorizes the socioeconomic status of Census tracts yearly on a scale from 1 to 4 based on American Community Survey data and elementary school performance data. Tier 1 Census tracts tend to be the lowest income, while Tier 4 Census tracts are highest income. Throughout this report, we conduct analyses for students of different subgroups, breaking information down by race/ethnicity and neighborhood tier. **Table A.1** shows the relationship between student race/ethnicity and CPS's neighborhood tiers. Round 1 applicants living in Tier 1 neighborhoods are 49 percent Latino and 48 percent Black, compared with Tier 4 neighborhoods where applicants are 31 percent Latino and 16 percent Black. This table provides a sense of the correlation between student race/ethnicity and neighborhood SES.

Table A.2 shows the characteristics of the applicant students based on their Round 1 offer and acceptance status. Specifically, we compare the characteristics of all Round 1 GoCPS applicants to subsets who accepted their offer (or not) and who did not receive an offer.

Among the applicants in Round 1, 65 percent accepted either their choice or SEHS program offer, and 11 percent accepted another program to which they were entitled to enroll such as the general education program at their neighborhood school. Relative to the students who accepted a choice or SEHS program offer, students who accepted a neighborhood or other option were more likely to be Latino (55 versus 48 percent), more likely to have had an IEP (18 vs. 13 percent), and had lower average NWEA math percentile scores (45 vs. 57) and lower average GPAs (2.6 vs. 2.9) than those students who accepted a choice or SEHS program offer.

Another 16 percent of applicants who received an offer either declined their offer or did not respond. The applicants who did not accept an initial offer in Round 1 also had lower average test scores and GPAs, were more likely to have had an IEP, were more likely to be Black or Other race, and were more likely to live in a Tier 4 neighborhood than applicants who accepted a choice or SEHS offer.

About 8 percent of applicants in Round 1 did not receive either a choice or SEHS program offer, although many were waitlisted for choice programs from which they may have received a later offer. The characteristics of these students are shown in the final column of **Table A.2**. On average, the students who did not receive an initial offer had higher math test scores and higher GPAs than Round 1 applicants who did receive initial offers. They were also less likely to be Latino or Black and more likely to live in a Tier 4 neighborhood. These students tended to list fewer programs on their application and to rank programs that were in higher demand, lessening their chances of receiving an offer. Additionally, these students were more likely to have attended eighth grade outside of CPS, suggesting that they might be more likely to enroll in an outside option.

TABLE A.1
Distribution of Student Race/Ethnicity by Neighborhood Tier

Student Race/Ethnicity	Tier 1	Tier 2	Tier 3	Tier 4
Latino	49%	57%	46%	31%
Black	48%	34%	35%	16%
White	1%	2%	8%	34%
Other	2%	6%	11%	19%

Note: Tier 1 Census tracts are relatively low-SES neighborhoods, while Tier 4 Census tracts are relatively high-SES neighborhoods. The "Other" race/ethnicity category includes Asian students, multi-race/ethnicity students, and students who are missing race/ethnicity information which is disproportionately true for applicants not enrolled in CPS for 8th grade. Percentages may not add up to 100 due to rounding.

TABLE A.2
Characteristics of Students by Initial Offer and Acceptance Status

Student Characteristic	All Round 1 Applicants	Accepted Choice or SEHS Program Offer	Accepted Other Program Offer	Did Not Accept an Initial Offer	Did Not Receive an Initial Offer
Tier 1	27%	29%	26%	26%	15%
Tier 4	19%	17%	16%	20%	32%
Latino	46%	48%	55%	38%	39%
Black	34%	34%	32%	40%	20%
White	9%	9%	8%	8%	13%
Other Race/Ethnicity	11%	8%	5%	15%	28%
Female	51%	52%	51%	46%	49%
IEP	14%	13%	18%	17%	10%
English Learner	9%	9%	13%	10%	6%
Math NWEA Percentile	54.4	57.3	45.5	46.3	58.9
GPA	2.8	2.9	2.6	2.5	3.0
Number of Choice Programs Ranked in Round 1	7.4	7.9	8.0	7.3	1.9
Participate in Round 2	15%	11%	17%	27%	23%
Number of Students	26,519	17,347	2,867	4,264	2,041

Note: Tier 1 Census tracts are relatively low-SES neighborhoods, while tier 4 Census tracts are relatively high-SES neighborhoods. The "Other race/ethnicity" category includes Asian students, multi-race/ethnicity students, and students who are missing race/ethnicity information. Some information is missing for non-applicants. Math NWEA test scores and GPA are calculated from seventh grade, which is used for admission to programs with test score or grade requirements.

ABOUT THE AUTHORS

LISA BARROW is an Affiliated Researcher at the UChicago Consortium, studying the high school application process and, in particular, the effectiveness of selective enrollment high schools. She is also working in partnership with the UChicago Consortium on an evaluation of efforts in Chicago Public Schools (CPS) to expand student access and enrollment in computer science courses. Lisa is a Senior Economist at the Federal Reserve Bank of Chicago. Her research focuses on issues in education, public finance, and labor economics. She has worked on a variety of issues in education, including a randomized evaluation of computer-aided algebra instruction in large urban school districts, evaluation of performance-based scholarships at the community college level (with MDRC), and follow-up and time use survey development for the MDRC PBS demonstration.

THE FEDERAL RESERVE BANK OF CHICAGO is one of 12 regional Reserve Banks that, along with the Board of Governors in Washington, DC, make up the nation's central bank. The Chicago Reserve Bank serves the seventh Federal Reserve District, which encompasses the northern portions of Illinois and Indiana, southern Wisconsin, the Lower Peninsula of Michigan, and the state of Iowa. In addition to participation in the formulation of monetary policy, each Reserve Bank supervises member banks and bank holding companies, provides financial services to depository institutions and the U.S. government, and monitors economic conditions in its District.

FEDERAL RESERVE BANK OF CHICAGO

LAUREN SARTAIN is a Senior Research Analyst at the UChicago Consortium. Her main research interests are in understanding policies and practices that urban schools can implement in order to improve the outcomes and lives of the students and adults in the public school system. To answer these kinds of policy-relevant research questions, she implements a variety of econometric and quasi-experimental research techniques with large-scale administrative data in order to hone in on the effects of various policies. Lauren has also worked at various research institutes like the Chapin Hall Center for Children and the Federal Reserve Bank of Chicago. She has published and presented on a wide range of topics, including teacher quality, school choice and school quality, and discipline reform. While Lauren believes it is critical to apply rigorous methods to answer important policy questions, strong research only goes so far. Being able to take key findings and communicate them in a way that is meaningful for families, practitioners, and policymakers is also essential and at the heart of the research-practice partnership model. Lauren's research at the UChicago Consortium gives her a unique vantage point from which to study real-world policy problems in an interdisciplinary way.

THE UNIVERSITY OF CHICAGO CONSORTIUM ON SCHOOL RESEARCH conducts research of high technical quality that can inform and assess policy and practice in the Chicago Public Schools. We seek to expand communication among researchers, policymakers, and practitioners as we support the search for solutions to the problems of school reform. The UChicago Consortium encourages the use of research in policy action and improvement of practice, but does not argue for particular policies or programs. Rather, we help to build capacity for school reform by identifying what matters for student success and school improvement, creating critical indicators to chart progress, and conducting theory-driven evaluation to identify how programs and policies are working. The UChicago Consortium is a unit of the Urban Education Institute.

UCHICAGO Consortium on School Research

This report reflects the interpretation of the authors. Although the UChicago Consortium's Steering Committee provided technical advice, no formal endorsement by these individuals, organizations, or the full Consortium should be assumed.

UCHICAGO Consortium on School Research

Directors

ELAINE M. ALLENSWORTH
Lewis-Sebring Director

CAMILLE A. FARRINGTON
Managing Director and Senior Research Associate

HOLLY HART
Survey Director

JENNY NAGAOKA
Deputy Director

MELISSA RODERICK
Senior Director
Hermon Dunlap Smith Professor
School of Social Service Administration

LISA SALL
Director of Outreach and Communication

PENNY BENDER SEBRING
Co-Founder

MARISA DE LA TORRE
Managing Director and Senior Research Associate

Steering Committee

RAQUEL FARMER-HINTON
Co-Chair
University of Wisconsin, Milwaukee

LUISIANA MELÉNDEZ
Co-Chair
Erikson Institute

Institutional Members

SARAH DICKSON
Chicago Public Schools

BRENDA DIXON
Illinois State Board of Education

ELIZABETH KIRBY
Chicago Public Schools

TROY LARAVIERE
Chicago Principals and Administrators Association

JESSE SHARKEY
Chicago Teachers Union

Individual Members

KATHLEEN CALIENTO
The Academy Group

GINA CANEVA
Lindblom Math & Science

NANCY CHAVEZ
OneGoal

JAHMAL COLE
My Block, My Hood, My City

KATIE HILL
City of Chicago

MEGAN HOUGARD
Chicago Public Schools

GREG JONES
The Academy Group

PRANAV KOTHARI
Revolution Impact, LLC

AMANDA LEWIS
University of Illinois at Chicago

RITO MARTINEZ
Surge Institute

SHAZIA MILLER
NORC at the University of Chicago

MICHELLE MORALES
Mikva Challenge

CRISTINA PACIONE-ZAYAS
Erikson Institute

PAIGE PONDER
One Million Degrees

REBECCA VONDERLACK-NAVARRO
Latino Policy Forum

PAM WITMER
Office of the Mayor, City of Chicago

JOHN ZEIGLER
DePaul University

www.ingramcontent.com/pod-product-compliance
Lightning Source LLC
Chambersburg PA
CBHW040033050426
42453CB00003B/101